An Essay on the Art of Ingeniously Tormenting

Jane Collier

Publish'd Jan.ʳ 1ˢᵗ 1800, by W. Miller, Old Bond Street.

AN
ESSAY
ON THE ART OF
INGENIOUSLY TORMENTING;
WITH
PROPER RULES
FOR THE
EXERCISE OF THAT AMUSING STUDY.

HUMBLY ADDRESSED,

PART I. TO THE MASTER, HUSBAND, &c.

PART II. TO THE WIFE, FRIEND, &c.

WITH SOME

GENERAL INSTRUCTIONS FOR PLAGUING ALL YOUR ACQUAINTANCE.

——Speak daggers—but use none.—SHAKSPEARE.

LONDON:

PRINTED FOR ANDREW MILLAR, IN THE STRAND, 1753;

REPRINTED FOR WILLIAM MILLER, IN OLD BOND-STREET,

By W. Bulmer and Co. Cleveland-row.

1804.

TO THE

HONOURABLE MRS ..... :

THE INGENIOUS TORMENTOR OF THE
PRESENT AGE.

————————

MADAM,

As the great business of high life now con-
sists in the Art *of ingeniously tormenting,*
and as you are acknowledged to excel so
pre-eminently in that science, I have taken
the liberty to offer this little volume to
your notice: trusting that you will some-
times place it in the·private pocket of your
vis-à-vis; that you will take especial care it
is regularly laid on the satin-wood table in
your boudoir; and also will give your orders

that it shall always appear on the salver, with the cakes, the comfitures, the milk-punch, and other restoratives, by means of which you, and your Friends, are enabled to endure the fatigue and ennui of fashionable society.

I have the honour to remain,

MADAM,

your Sylph, and Friend,

THE INVISIBLE GIRL.

ADVERTISEMENT

OF THE PRESENT EDITOR.

MISS JANE COLLIER, the Authoress of the present work, was the eldest sister of Dr. Collier of the Commons; who was the intimate friend of the celebrated Fielding, and his sister Sarah. The Essay dates its commencement from a party, in which her brother was present; who often lamented, that a sister possessing such amiable manners, and such abilities, should only be known to the literary world by a satirical work.

I wish, however, to preserve all the monuments of female genius; and though I lament, with her brother, that *Miss Collier* did not give a more varied, or extended scope to her literary powers, I must acknowledge that, amidst the innumerable talents of the fair sex, they possess the talent of ridicule in an eminent degree.—

ADVERTISEMENT.

Of the history of our Authoress; little has survived : she enjoyed the friendship and confidence of *Richardson ;* and probably among the number of his female characters, that of *Miss Collier* was pourtrayed. Both herself, and her friend *Miss Sarah Fielding*, were excellent Greek and Latin scholars, and received their education equally from Dr. Collier.

Miss J. Collier's father was rector of *Langford* in Wiltshire : her sister *Margaret* accompanied Fielding to *Lisbon*, and though not mentioned by name in his Journey thither, she is alluded to in that account. Miss *Collier* had a brother, who was a colonel in the army.

J. S. C.

CONTENTS.

PART I.

CHAPTER I.

CHAPTER II.

CHAPTER III.

CHAPTER IV.

CONTENTS.

PART II.

CHAPTER I.

ESSAY

ON THE

ART OF TORMENTING.

ENGLAND has ever been allowed to excel most other nations in her improvements of arts and sciences, although she seldom claims to herself the merit of invention: to her improvements also are many of her neighbours indebted, for the exercise of some of their most useful arts.

It is not the benefit that may arise to the few from any invention, but its general utility, which ought to make such invention of universal estimation. Had the art of navigation gone no higher than to direct the course of a small boat by oars, the Low Countries only could have been the better for it. Again, should the inhabitants of Lapland invent the most convenient method for warming their houses by stoves, bringing them, by their improvements, to the utmost perfection; yet could not those who live within the tropics receive the least benefit from such their improvements; any more than the Laplanders could, from the invention of fans, umbrellas, and cooling grottos.

But as the science recommended in this short Essay will be liable to no such exceptions; being, we presume, adapted to the circumstances, genius, and capacity of every nation under Heaven, why should I doubt of that deserved fame, generally given to those

Inventas aut qui vitam excoluere per artes,
Quique sui memores alios fecere merendo?

VIRG. l. vi. v. 663.

That are found, or the person who improved life through science and art. And those who have made others mindful of gaining merit?

unless, indeed, I should be told, that mankind are already too great adepts in this art, to need any farther instructions.

May I hope that my dear countrymen will pardon me for presuming (by the very publication of these rules) that they are not already absolutely perfect in this our art? Or at least, that they may not always have an ingenious torment ready at hand to inflict?

By the common run of servants, it might have been presumed, that Dean Swift's instructions to them were unnecessary: but I dare believe no one ever read over that ingenious work, without finding there some inventions for idleness, carelessness, and ill-behaviour, which had never happened within his own experience.

Although I do not suppose mankind in general to be thorough proficients in this our art; yet wrong not my judgment so much, gentle reader, as to imagine, that I would write *institutes* of any science, to those who are unqualified for its practice, or do not shew some genius in themselves towards it. Should you observe in one child a delight of drawing, in another a turn towards music, would you not do your utmost to assist their genius, and to further their attempts? It is the great progress that I have observed to be already made in this our pleasant art, and the various attempts that I daily see towards bringing it to perfection, that encouraged me to offer this my poor assistance.

One requisite for approbation, I confess, is wanting in this work; for, alas! I fear it will contain nothing new. But what is wanting in novelty, shall be made up in utility; for, although I may not be able to shew one new and untried method of plaguing, teazing, or tormenting; yet will it not be a very great help to any one, to have all the best and most approved methods collected together in one small pocket volume? Did I promise a new set of rules, then, whatever was not mine, might be claimed by its proper owner; and, like the jay in the fable, I should justly be stripped of my borrowed plumes: but, as I declare myself only an humble collector, I doubt not but every one, who has practised, or who in writing has described, an ingenious torment, will thank me for putting it into this my curious collection.

That a love to this science is implanted in our natures, or early inculcated, is very evident, from the delight many children take in teazing and tormenting little dogs, cats, squirrels, or any other harmless animal, that they get into their power.

This love of tormenting may be said to have one thing in common with what, some writers affirm, belongs to the true love of virtue; namely, that it is exercised for its own sake, and no other: for, can there be a clearer proof, that, for its own

sake alone, this art of tormenting is practised, than that it never did, nor ever can,
answer any other end? I know that the
most expert practitioners deny this; and
frequently declare, when they whip, cut,
and slash the body, or when they teaze,
vex, and torment the mind, that it is done
for the good of the person that suffers.
Let the vulgar believe this if they will;
but I, and my good pupils, understand
things better; and while we can enjoy the
high pleasure of tormenting, it matters
not what the objects of our power either
feel, think, or believe.

With what contempt may we, adepts
in this science, look down on the tyrants
of old! On Nero, Caligula, Phalaris, and
all such paltry pretenders to our art!
Their inventions ending in death, freed
the sufferer from any farther torments;
or, if they extended only to broken bones,
and bodily wounds, they were such as the
skill of the surgeon could rectify or heal:

but where is the hand can cure the wounds of unkindness, which our ingenious artists inflict?

The practice of tormenting the body is not now, indeed, much allowed, except in some particular countries, where slavery and ignorance subsist: but let us not, my dear countrymen, regret the loss of that trifling branch of our power, since we are at full liberty to exercise ourselves in that much higher pleasure, the tormenting the mind. Nay, the very laws themselves, although they restrain us from being too free with our bastinado, pay so much regard to this our strong desire of tormenting, that, in some instances, they give us the fairest opportunities we could wish, of legally indulging ourselves in this pleasant sport.

To make myself clearly understood, examine the case, as it stands (if I mistake not) between the debtor and creditor.

If a person owes me a thousand pounds

(which perhaps, too, may be my all), and has an estate of yearly that value, he may, if he pleases, and has a mind to plague, distress, and vex me, refuse paying me my money. Arrest him, then, cry you.—— If he be not in Parliament, I do——He gives bail; and, with my own money, works me through all the quirks of the law.——At last (if he be of the true blood of those my best disciples, who would hang themselves to spite their neighbours) he retires into the liberties of the Fleet, or King's Bench; lives at his ease, and laughs at me and my family, who are starving. However, as some inconveniences attend such a proceeding, this method of plaguing a creditor is not very often practised.

But on the other hand, how can I be thankful enough to our good laws, for indulging me in the pleasure of persecuting and tormenting a man who is indebted to me, and who does not want the WILL, but the POWER, to pay me!

As soon as I perceive this to be the case, I instantly throw him in gaol, and there I keep him to pine away his life in want and misery.—How will my pleasure be increased, if he should be a man in any business or profession! for I then rob him of all probable means of escaping my power. It may be objected, perhaps, that in this last instance I act imprudently; that I defeat my own ends, and am myself the means of my losing my whole money. —How ignorant of the true joys of tormenting is such an objector! You mistake greatly, my friend, if you think I defeat my own ends;—for my ends are to plague and torment, not only a fellow-creature, but a fellow-christian.—And are there not instances enough of this kind of practice, to make us fairly suppose, that the value of one thousand, or ten thousand pounds, is nothing, compared to the excessive delight of tormenting?

But let me raise this joyous picture a

little higher.—Let me suppose, that this wretched man, now pining in a prison, has a wife and children, whom he fondly loves——Must not my pleasure be doubled and trebled by the consideration, that his children are starving; that his wife is in the same condition, oppressed also with unspeakable anguish for not being able to give her helpless infants any relief?—Suppose, too, that the husband, with the reflection of all this, and his own incapacity to help them, should be driven to distraction! would not this exceed the most malicious transports of revenge ever exercised by an antient or modern tyrant?

If there are some odd sort of people, who have no great relish for this kind of happiness, which I have here attempted to describe; yet let them not hastily condemn it, as unnatural: for I appeal to the experience of mankind, and ask—Whether there is any one who has not heard of, at least, one instance of distress, near

as high as the scene before described?
And that the love of tormenting must
have been the sole motive to a creditor's
acting in such a manner, when his debtor
could not pay him, is evident, from the
impossibility of reasonably assigning any
other cause.

One strong objection, I know, will be
made against my whole design, by people
of weak consciences; which is, that every
rule I shall lay down will be exactly
opposite to the doctrine of Christianity.
Greatly, indeed, in a Christian country,
should I fear the force of such an objection, could I perceive that any one vice
was refrained from on that account only.
Both theft and murder are forbidden by
God himself: yet can any one say, that
our lives and properties would be in the
least secure; were it not for the penal
laws of our country? Who is there, that
having received a blow on one cheek, will
turn the other, while revenge can be had

from the law of assault and battery? Are
there any who exercise the virtues of patience and forgiveness, if they can have
legal means of punishing the aggressor,
and revenging themselves tenfold on the
person who gives them the most slight
offence? Innumerable are the instances
that could be given to shew, that the doctrine of the Gospel has very little influence
upon the practice of its *followers*; unless
it be on a few obscure people, that *nobody
knows*. The foregoing formidable objection, therefore, we hope, is pretty well got
over, except with the *obscure few* above-
mentioned.

But as I would willingly remove every
the least shadow of an objection that I
am acquainted with, I must take notice
of one which was made by a person very
zealous indeed for our cause; but who
feared, he said, that people would not bear
publicly to avow their love of tormenting,
and their disregard of that very religion

which they profess. This, at first, almost staggered me, and I was going to throw by my work, till I recollected several books (some too written by divines) that had been extremely well received, although they struck at the very foundation of our religion. These precedents are surely sufficient to make me depend upon coming off with impunity, let me publish what I will, except a libel against any great man. For to abuse Christ himself is not, at present, esteemed so high an offence, as to abuse one of his followers; or, rather, one of his ABUSERS; for such may we term all those, who, without observing his laws, call themselves after his name.

It has been already observed, that the torments of the body are not much allowed in civilized nations: but yet, under the notion of punishments for faults, such as whipping and picketing amongst the soldiers; with some sorts of curious marine discipline, as the cat-of-nine-tails, keel-hawling, and the like; a man may pick out some excellent fun; for if he will now-and-then inflict those punishments on the good, which were intended for the chastisement and amendment of the bad, he will not only work the flesh, but vex the spirit, of an ingenuous youth; as nothing can be more grating to a liberal mind, than to be so unworthily treated.

If I should be so happy, my good pupils, by these my hearty endeavours, as to instruct you thoroughly in the ingenious art of plaguing and tormenting the mind, you will have also more power over the body than you are at first aware of. You may take the Jew's* forfeit of a pound of flesh, without incurring the imputation of barbarity which was cast on him for that diverting joke. He was a mere mongrel at tormenting, to think of cutting it off with a knife; no—your true delicate way

* See the Merchant of Venice, written by Shakspeare.

is to waste it off by degrees.—For has not every creditor (by the pleasant assistance of a prison) the legal power of taking ten or twenty pounds of Christian flesh, in forfeit of his bond ?

However, without such violent measures, you may have frequent opportunities (by teazing and tormenting) of getting out of your friends a good pretty picking. But be very careful daily to observe, whether your patient continues in good health, and is fat and well-liken: if so, you may be almost certain, that your whole labour is thrown away. As soon, therefore, as you perceive this to be the case, you must (to speak in the phrase of surgeons, when they hack and hue a human body) immediately choose another SUBJECT.

ESSAY

ON THE

ART OF TORMENTING.

PART I.

PART I.

THE following instructions are divided into Two Parts. This First Part is addressed to those, who may be said to have an exterior power from visible authority, such as is vested, by law or custom, in masters over their servants; parents over their children; husbands over their wives; and many others. The Second Part will be addressed to those, who have an interior power, arising from the affection of the person on whom they are to work; as in the case of the wife, the friend, &c.

It would be tiresome, and almost endless, to enumerate every connexion under

the two foregoing heads: I have therefore
taken only a few of the principal ones in
each division; and shall begin with masters and mistresses, as in the following
Chapter.

CHAPTER I.

Instructions to Masters and Mistresses, concerning their Servants.

As the intercourse between a master and his man is not so frequent as between a lady and her maid, I shall not direct myself to the former, but only give rules to the latter; and where those rules are practicable for the master, I hope he will be so kind as to convert them to his own use.

To scold at and torment *all* your servants, appears, at first sight, to be the desirable thing; but those who study the best method of this amusing art, will tell you, that it is much better to select out one or two, at the most, who are proper objects, and who you are sure can feel your strokes; for by this means you may make use of all your bad servants, as instruments to plague the good.

Be sure on no account to make use of any distinction, or ever examine into the true author of any fault or carelessness, unless it be done privately, in order to lay the blame on a wrong person; as for instance;

If you blame Susan the house-maid for having done such a thing, and she should say, " Indeed, madam, it was not I, but " Martha the cook, that did it;" you must raise your voice, and tell her, that you cannot trouble your head to distinguish amongst such low wretches—that *all* servants are careless alike; and if you have any more such accidents in your family, they shall *all* go.

If, on blaming any servant for a fault, she should be able to excuse herself, in a manner that ought to be perfectly satisfactory to a reasonable person, you have nothing for it, but to say, that you will not hear the impertinent discourse of such a wench—that if she cannot hold her tongue, she is no servant for you—and that you never knew a servant guilty of a fault, but had pertness and invention enough to make a good excuse for it— then lament, that you do not live in a country, where you might be so happy as to be served by mutes.

Be sure never to lay the saddle upon the right horse, as being the most certain method of galling.

The old saying,

> Twice I did well, and that I heard never;
> Once I did ill, and that I heard ever;

must by no means be contradicted by *you*; for the oftener you give your servants an opportunity to apply it to themselves, the oftener do you make them feel your power.

The two foregoing rules are of general use to all your friends and acquaintance.

When your servants are sick, you may

in earnest be very kind and good to them, as it will greatly contribute towards gaining you the reputation of good-nature, and as it is necessary for your own convenience to restore them to health, in order to make them useful. Besides, you may use them ten times the worse for it when they are well, and perpetually upbraid them with your kindness to them when they were ill. As servants, by their way of life, are generally pretty healthy, you need not fear that this practice will go very deep towards exhausting your stock of kindness; for you must take care to have a watchful eye, not to be imposed on by sham sickness; and if a servant falls into a lingering disorder, you have nothing to do but directly to turn them away.

When you hire a footman, be sure to insist upon it, that he pays so strict a regard to your orders, and your *way* in doing every thing, that the least deviation in any point should be a forfeit of his place.

This gives frequent opportunities for rating and scolding; for it is but to make your orders impracticable, and then, be sure not to hear one word they can say in their defence, for not having performed impossibilities. Or you may lay several traps, to tempt them not to adhere strictly to your commands, and make it a matter of offence, whether they do, or do not.

To explain myself in this, let me give you an instance:

If you go to visit a friend, in a showery day, when the weather is quite uncertain, you may order your footman to come for you at such an hour, and bid him come without the coach, for you would walk home. If the weather should prove fair, you must for that day lose your diversion: but if it rains, then your sport begins. Should your man (thinking it impossible for you to choose walking in the wet and dirt), contrary to your orders, bring you the coach, you may rate him extremely for not observing your orders. You may tell him, that you did not want his care for your health, nor his wisdom to comment on your directions—that all you wanted in a servant was obedience—that you would not, for an hundred guineas, have had your horses brought out in such a wet evening. If you are in London, you may say you intended to take a chair; but if you are in the country, you must declare, that you would rather have walked home two miles through the rain, than have had your poor horses so cruelly exposed: but it was your misfortune to have such wise people about you, that they did not think you knew how to give your own orders.

On the other hand, should the footman, fearful of disobeying your commands, come to you in this wet evening, without the coach; then may you lament your hard fate, in having nothing but fools about you, that could not distinguish in common occurrences.

If you can once catch a servant in this, or any such-like trap, it gives continual new opportunities of scolding. For if the fault was the adherence to your commands, you may always to your orders add—" But pray remember, I am not " such a tyrant and a fool, as you sup- " posed me when you made me walk " home in the wet." And if his fault was the departing from the strict letter of your commands; then to your orders you may add—" But pray mind what I say to you, " and not go according to your own wis- " dom, as you did when you gave my " horses cold by bringing them out in the " rain."

If you have no children, keep as large a quantity of tame animals as you conveniently can. If you have children, a smaller number will do. Shew the most extravagant fondness, you possibly can, for all these animals. Let them be of the most troublesome and mischievous sort, such as cats, monkeys, parrots, squirrels, and little snarling lap-dogs. Their uses for the tormenting your servants are various. In the first place, if they are properly encouraged, and never tamed, they will be so liberal of their teeth and claws, that the servants will, in general, be bit and scratched all over. Then, if any servant should dare to offend one of these favourites, there is a noble field for scolding and rating them: and one farther use, and not one of the least, of these animals, is to feed them with all sorts of rarities, and give them (I mean the dogs and cats) what your servants would be glad of, while you feed them with the coarsest and cheapest diet that you can get.

If you happen to have a very good cook, you must strictly enquire into her

temper; and if you find her a termagant
(as most cooks are, according to Ben.
Jonson's observation), you must give up
all hopes of plaguing *her*. You must then
find your enjoyment in the good dinners
she dresses for you, and the use she will
be of to oppress the other servants. If
she should be ever so good a cook, and
should happen to be good-tempered, you
must not let her escape you, but must
always send her down word, that your
dinner was not eatable. It is true, indeed,
that, by this means, you may make her
leave her place, and you may lose a good
servant: but you are no true lover of the
noble game of tormenting, if a good dinner, or any other convenience or enjoyment, can give you half the pleasure, as
the teazing and mortifying a good indus-
trious servant, who has done her very best
to please you.

But to return to my termagant cook.
—When you have such an one, then

remember you have a jewel. In the first place, make a favourite of her; for be it observed always, that the very worst amongst your servants is to be your greatest favourite.

Hearken to all the stories she has a mind to tell you, of the rest of the servants; and if any complaint is made against her, say you disbelieve it; adding, that you perceive they are all in a plot against poor Martha the cook; and that they have a mind to distress you, by endeavouring to make you part with the *only* good servant you have; besides intending, you suppose, to poison you with some slut of their own recommending.

Your house-maid you have so little intercourse with, that I hardly know how to direct your proceedings with regard to her. If you love a clean house, keep a good house-maid, when you can get one; but enquire also concerning her temper. If it is very bad, be sure not to part with

her, as she will contribute towards plague-
ing the other servants: but if she be a
very good-natured obliging girl, and ready
to assist her fellow-servants, you may
teaze her about the dirtiness of the house,
as I directed with regard to the good-
natured cook about her dinners, till you
have sent her packing; and you may
chance, perhaps, to have better luck with
the next.

Scolding at all the servants, as before
observed, is too common and vulgar a
method; nor is it ever used by your true
adepts in the art of tormenting. But some
pretty good proficients in the science have
made a favourite of their own maid, and
made her the insolent instrument of wor-
rying the rest. This is a tolerable good
method, but, in my opinion, not the very
best. To know that all the lower part of
your family are persecuted and plagued
by a taunting creature of your own tutor-
ing, is a pleasant reflection; but yields

not half the joy as bringing the game nearer home. If you have a husband, or friend, a toad-eater, or some grown up children, to exercise your talents on, you may proceed in the above beaten path, as having work enough already on your hands; and you may then be contented to execute your torments on your lower servants, by suffering that proxy, your own woman, to worry them: but if you have none of the before-mentioned subjects, then most excellent sport will be found from teazing and vexing your own maid, which may be done in the following manner:

Let us suppose, that you have just hired Mrs. Jenny to be about your own person: suppose her, also, to be a clean, well-looking, good-natured girl. Be very kind to her for about a week, that you may raise her expectations of leading an easy, quiet life; for in a judicious disappointment lies half the art in every connection

whatever. When Jenny is satisfied, by
your kind behaviour, that you are very
well disposed towards her, begin some
familiar discourse with her; and draw her
on to a freedom of speech, that, without
such encouragement, would never have
come into her head: then fly all at once
into a violent rage with her; call her
saucy, pert, and impudent; upbraid her
with being sprung from a dunghill, and
blame yourself for conversing with so
low a wretch.

Always scold at her, if she is the least
undressed or dirty; and say you cannot
bear such beasts about you.

If she is clean and well-dressed, tell
her, that you suppose she dresses out for
the fellows; for the wenches of this age
are so forward, that the men can hardly
be quiet for them.

Order her to call you in a morning,
and, although she comes in ever so softly,
fall into a violent passion, because she

made such a noise, as to start you suddenly out of your sleep.

If she ever does any thing extremely well to please you; as wash your finest lace, or make up your cap, &c. you may commend her very highly for it,—once, but no more.—For you must on no account ever afterward fail to find fault with her, although it be done ever so well. And always, to your finding fault, add a reproach, how well it was done such a time; and how much you then commended her for it; but commendations and praises ever spoil the best servant in the world; it was owing, you may say, to the baseness and ingratitude of servants, that you was forced to put a restraint upon your own natural temper, which prompted you to all sorts of kindness and indulgences: yet your hard case was such, that you could not so much as commend a wench for ironing a cap, but she presently grew careless, and good for nothing, upon it.

Remember always to teaze and sooth her so alternately, that she shall be vastly puzzled, whether to be pleased or displeased with her place: but, whenever you have been pretty free with your torments, you must talk of leaving off some old gown, or of some great persons coming to your house; or in some other manner endeavour to awaken her interest, so that she may not leave you.

When you are in high good-humour and familiarity with her, you may say, " That you are not one of those mistresses " who never think of diverting their poor " servants; and that you intend, there- " fore, the next day, to take her abroad " with you: if in London, to see sights, " &c. or if in the country, to walk, or go " upon the water with you; or any other " way that may come into your head." Your condescension, in making her your companion, will greatly elate her spirits; and your kindness will fill her heart with

grateful pleasure. You cannot rob her of
the joy she will have in the expectation of
this promised favour; but the higher that
is raised, the greater will be her disappointment, when the next morning you contrive to keep her so fully employed, till the
moment you are setting out, that it will
be impossible for her to get herself ready:
then fly into the highest rage imaginable
with her, for making you wait; but by no
means leave her behind; for that stroke
she will soon recover by amusing herself
with her fellow-servants, and being rid of
your scolding; take her therefore with
you; and lecture her all the way, on her
baseness and ingratitude, in plaguing you
in such a manner, in return for your intended kindness. Don't suffer her, the
whole day, to look up, or say her very soul
is her own: so that in the midst of this
pleasant expedition, taken, as you may
tell her, by you, out of pure good-nature,
to please a dirty wench, she may wish to

her soul that she was at home, either in the wash-house or the scullery, performing the most laborious offices in the lowest station in the family.

But let us suppose the patience of your miserable object quite exhausted, and that she is worked into a proper indifference about pleasing you; so that you should find that she minded very little what you said to her; only (considering yours as a profitable place) that she was resolved to bear all your tricks, for the sake of your money; then part with her directly, and get another: for all the pleasure of tormenting is lost, as soon as your subject is become insensible to your strokes.

CHAPTER II.

To the Patronesses of an humble Companion.

I HAVE often wondered, considering the great number of families there are, whose fortunes are so large, that the addition of one, or even two, would hardly be felt, that they should not more frequently take into their houses, and under their protection, young women who have been well educated; and who, by the misfortune or death of their friends, have been left destitute of all means of subsistence. There are many methods for young men, in the like circumstances, to acquire a genteel maintenance; but for a girl, I know not of one way of support, that does not, by the custom of the world, throw her below the rank of a gentlewoman.

There are two motives for taking such young women under protection.

One is, the pleasure which (it is said) kind and benevolent hearts must take in relieving from distress one of their fellow-creatures; and, for their repeated kindness and indulgence to such, receiving the daily tribute of grateful assiduity, and cheerful looks. For I have been informed, by a person well versed in human nature, that, however loud the outcry is against ingratitude for real kindness, yet that true and real kindness seldom or never did excite ingratitude: and moreover, that when those violent outcries came to be examined into, the obliged person had, in fact, been guilty of no ingratitude, or the patron had bestowed no real kindness. Nay, farther, that, should it be proved, that ungrateful returns are sometimes made for real favours, it would commonly be found, upon inquiry, that the persons conferring such favours had a blind side open to flattery, or some other passion; by which means they had shut their eyes, and plucked a poisonous weed to place in their bosoms, instead of using their power of sight and distinction, in order to gather one of those many grateful flowers, which nature has scattered over the face of the earth: the intoxicating quality of which weed has still kept their eyes closed, till they are roused by some racking pain, which it instils into the inmost recesses of the heart.

But, notwithstanding the before-mentioned outcry against ingratitude, there are some, I must confess, who, from compassion and generosity, have taken the distressed into their protection, and have treated them with the highest kindness and indulgence. Nay, I have known a set of tasteless, silly people, who are so void of any relish for this our pleasant game, that they would never wish to see a face in sorrow or tears, unless it was in their power to dry those tears, and turn that sorrow into cheerful smiles. But to such insipid folks I write not; as I know my rules, to them, would be of little service. I address myself, therefore, in this chapter, only to those who take young women into their houses, as new subjects of their power.

From the dejection that is so often seen in the countenances of those that live dependent; from Cowley's exclamation against that state, as being the thing that he would wish to his most bitter enemy; from the anxiety that people shew, to possess fortune enough to render themselves independent; may we not infer, that there are many patronesses, who have a true relish for this sport, and who will thank me for these my rules? For although this little book may not help them to one new and untried method of tormenting; yet it may keep the old ones ready in their minds, to be exerted on all proper occasions.

There is some difficulty in giving rules for tormenting a dependent, that shall differ from those already laid down for plaguing and teazing your servants, as the two stations differ so very little in themselves. The servant, indeed, differs in this; she receives wages, and the humble companion receives none: the servant is most part of the day out of your sight; the humble companion is always ready at hand to receive every cross word that rises in your mind: the servants can be teazed only by yourself, your dogs, your cats, your parrots, your children; the humble companion, besides being the sport of all these, must, if you manage rightly, bear the insults of all your servants themselves; who, the worse you use them, will the more readily use the power you give them, of revenging themselves on poor Miss Lucy ———.

In the first place, let me advise you to be very careful in the choice of an humble companion; for be it always remembered, that, in every connection where this art of teazing and tormenting is exercised, much depends upon the subject of your power.

In a servant, you have little to look for but diligence and good-nature; but in a dependent there are many more requisites.

Let her be well born, and well educated. The more acquirements she has, the greater field will you have for insolence, and the pleasure of mortifying her. Out of the numberless families in the church and army, that outlive themselves, and come to decay, great will be your choice. Pick out, if possible, one that has lived a happy life, under tender and indulgent parents. Beauty, or deformity; good sense, or the want of it; may any of them, with proper management, so well answer your purpose, that you need not be very curious as to that matter: but on no account take into your house one that has not a tender heart, with a meek and gentle disposition; for if she has spirit enough to despise your insults, and has not tender affections enough to be soothed and melted by your kindness (which must be sparingly bestowed), all your sport is lost; and you might as well shoot your venom at a marble statue in your garden.

Although I have supposed, that beauty or deformity, good sense or folly, in your dependent, are in some measure indifferent, yet I would have you, if possible, mix them thus: take good sense, with plainness or deformity; and beauty, with a very weak capacity.

If your humble companion be handsome, with no great share of understanding, observe the following directions towards Miss Kitty:

Take care seldom to call her any thing but *Beauty, Pretty Idiot, Puppet, Babyface*; with as many more of such sarcastical epithets as you can invent.

If you can ever provoke her enough to
shew any resentment in her countenance,
you may *beseech* her to spare her frowns
for those who will fear them; and keep
her disdainful looks for the footmen, when
they make love to her; which, by her
flirting airs, you make no doubt they are
encouraged to do. But if, by your discourse, you move her tears, you may call
her *Weeping beauty*; and ask her, out of
what play, or idle romance, she had learnt
that tears were becoming. Then drive her
out of the room with these words, " Be
" gone out of my sight, you blubbering
" fool—*Handsome indeed!* If I had a dog
" that looked so frightful, I would hang
" him."

Although you may, generally, insult
her with her beauty, yet be sure, at times,
to say so many mortifying things, as shall
make her believe you do not think her in
the least handsome. If her complexion
is fair, call her *Whey-face*; if it is not of

the whitest sort, you may tell her, she is
as brown as mahogany: if she is inclin-
able to pale, tell her she always looks as
white as a cloth: and you may add,
" That whatever people may fancy of
" their own sweet persons, yet, in your
" opinion, there could be no beauty in a
" whited wall." In this case, sometimes,
insultingly, the name of *Lily-face!* will
come in. If she has a fine bloom, tell her
she looks as red-faced, as if she drank
brandy; and you have no notion, you
may say, of cook-maid beauty. Thus, by
right management, every personal perfection may be turned to her reproach.
Fine large eyes may be accused of gog-
gling; small ones may be termed un-
meaning, and insignificant; and so of
every feature beside. But if she happens
to have fine, white, even teeth, you have
no resource, but to tell her, whenever you
catch her smiling, that she is mighty
fond of grinning, to shew her white teeth.

Then add, " Pray remember, child, that " you cannot shew your teeth, without " shewing your folly." You may likewise declare, that if you had a girl of your own, who shewed such a silly vanity, you would flay her alive.

. One thing be sure not to omit, although it is ever so false; which is, to tell her, and in the plainest and grossest terms, that she has (oh shocking accusation to a fine girl!)* sweaty feet, and a nauseous breath.

---

* To those who are displeased at the indelicacy of the above expression, with some others that follow, and would wish them omitted, I can only say, in the words of Butler a little altered,

And though some critic here cries shame,
And says our author is to blame,
                    HUD. Part i. Cant. ii. v. 379.
To such I answer, Cruel fate
Tells me thy counsel comes too late.
                    Cant. iii. v. 585.

Or, in plain prose, it is desired to be remembered, that it is the lady patroness, and not our author, that uses such coarse language.

To a young creature of beauty, and any degree of delicacy, nothing can be more teazing and grating to hear, than this. From the extreme mortification she must feel, it is ten to one but she will deny it, with some resentment, or will shed tears of vexation for the charge: these will both equally serve your purpose. If the first, you have many ways to deal with her. Furious scolding and abuse is no bad method, if not too lately practised; but insulting taunts, I think, will do rather better. Such as follow:

" Oh to be sure! you are too delicate a
" creature to have any human failings!
" you are all sweetness and perfection!
" well, Heaven defend me from such
" sweet creatures!" Then changing your tone and looks into fierceness, you may proceed: " I tell you, Madam Imperti-
" nence, whatever you may think, and
" how impudently soever you may dare
" to contradict me in this manner, that

" all your nasty odious imperfections, have
" been often taken notice of by many
" people besides myself, though nobody
" had regard enough for you, to tell you
" of such things.—You may toss your
" head, and look with as much indigna-
" tion as you please; but these airs, child,
" will not do long with me.—If you do
" not like to be told of your faults, you
" must find some other person to support
" you. So pray, for the present, walk off
" to your own apartment; and consider
" whether you choose to lay aside that
" pretty, becoming resentment of yours;
" or to be thrown friendless, as I found
" you, on the wide world again.—You
" must not be told of your failings, truly,
" must you! Oh I would not have such a
" proud heart as thine is in my breast, for
" the world! Though, let me tell you,
" Mistress Minx, it would much better
" become my station, than yours."

For fear this kind and gentle speech of

yours should have wounded too deeply;
and Miss Kitty should really, on consideration, prefer wandering, beggary, or
the most menial service, to such a life of
dependence, and you should thereby lose
your game, be sure not to let it be above
half an hour before you send your woman
up stairs to her, with some sweetmeats,
fruit, or any thing you know she is fond
of. Order your woman, if she finds her in
a rage, to soften her mind, till she brings
her to tears; then to comfort her; and
tell her how kindly you had been just then
talking of her; and to leave no means
untried to coax her down. You must
then receive her with the highest good-
humour; and tell her, you intend for her
some new cloaths, a pleasant jaunt, or
any indulgence, that you know would
please her: continue this good-humour so
strongly, that she shall not have the least
opportunity of telling you, what, undoubtedly, she must have resolved above stairs;

namely, that she could live with you no
longer. And if this fit of kindness be
carried into a proper excess, the poor girl
will, at last, begin to think herself to
blame; and that you are the kindest, best
creature to her in the world. Then is she
properly prepared for the next torment
you shall think fit to inflict.

Should Miss Kitty, on the mortifying
accusation before mentioned, burst into
tears, you must proceed in a contrary
method. You may wonder what should
make her cry, when you was only kindly
telling her, as a friend, of some misfortunes she could not help. You was far
(you may say) from blaming her; for although, you thanked Heaven, you was
free from all such shocking and disagreeable things yourself, yet nobody pitied
people with such imperfections more than
you did. You might here, also, aggravate
the misfortune it was, to so young and so
pretty a girl, to have such personal defects:

for (you may add) that you had often
heard the men declare (and you thought
them very much in the right), that they
should prefer the ugliest girl that ever
was born, who was sweet in her person, to
the greatest beauty upon earth, with such
nauseous, disgustful imperfections.

If Miss Kitty, in the midst of her sobs,
should find her voice enough to deny the
charge, you may go on as follows:

" I don't wonder, my dear, that you
" are not sensible of these things yourself;
" it is a very common case: but you
" should, therefore, take it more kind of
" those who will tell you of them.—Come,
" don't cry, my dear child, about it, any
" more: hearken to me; and I'll try to
" comfort you, if I can. You know, my
" love, I have often told you how dread-
" ful a situation a girl of your beauty
" would be in, should you lose my pro-
" tection: how many would be the snares
" then laid for your ruin! How likely is

" it, that, in time, you would be deserted
" by those base wretches your seducers!
" You know I have often wept, from my
" dreadful apprehensions for you, lest you
" should come to walk London streets.—
" But dry up your eyes; I have better
" hopes for you, Miss Kitty; for these
" ugly things I have been telling you of
" (and which, I assure you, are greatly
" taken notice of already) will, when they
" once come to be known, secure you
" more against the addresses of that de-
" stroyer man, than even extreme old age
" and ugliness."

With this jargon of insult, reproach,
and seeming tenderness, the girl's heart
will be ready to burst; nor will she be
able to form any kind of reply. You
may then continue the same farce; take
her by the hand; say you are sorry you
had even mentioned such things to her,
as your discourse seemed so much to affect her: bid her take care to change her

stockings very often, and not come too near you with her breath; and you would promise her, that you never would speak to her about either any more.

This promise remember strictly to keep: but yet you may take frequent opportunities of mortifying her, even in a room full of company; by vehemently inveighing against those very things of which you had accused her. You may go so far as to say, that you know an exceeding pretty girl, who has all those misfortunes; but you love her so, well, you would not, for the world, expose her by naming her name; yet, by kind nods upon Miss Kitty, the whole room will understand your meaning. You may also, whenever she comes near you, hastily take snuff, or smell to your sans-pareil; then look at her, rather with pity than any kind of anger; and, by this means, you may keep her in such a continual mortified state, that you will very seldom need any other strokes of your power: unless indeed she happens to receive any particular address from the young gentlemen who visit at your house, with due commendations of her person, and genteel appearance: which will, in all probability, so elate her mortified spirits, that you must have another trial of skill with her, to fetch her down.

So far for a handsome girl. But,

If plainness, with a good share of natural parts, should be the lot of this your dependent, whom we will call Miss Fanny, great scope will you have, in a different way, for tormenting, teazing, and plaguing her.

You must begin with all sorts of mortifying reflections on her person; and frequently declare, that you hate any thing about you that is not agreeable to look at. This, in the beginning, will vex the girl; first, as it is not very pleasant to have a mirror perpetually held to our view, where the reflection is so mortifying: and next, as she will really be sorry to find herself disagreeable to a person she would wish to please. But in time she will find you out: she will perceive the malice of such reflections; and, if she has good sense, will get above any concern about what you can say of her person. As soon as you perceive this, change your method; and level most of your darts against her understanding. Never let a day pass, without calling her, in that day, a WIT, at least a hundred times. Begin most requests, or rather commands, with these sort of phrases, " Will your Wisdom please " to do so or so, &c. Can a lady of your " fine parts condescend to darn this apron? " Would it not be too great a conde- " scension for a WIT, to submit to look " over my housekeeper's accounts?" Whatever answer she makes to these things; whether it be shewing a little resentment for such insolent treatment; or saying, with mildness, that she is ready to do any thing you command her; let your reply be—" I don't hear, child, what you say. " —However, I presume it was something " mighty smart and witty.—But let me " give you one piece of advice; which is, " to be more sparing of your tongue, and " less sparing of your labour, if you ex- " pect a continuance of my favour to " you——"

Although your chief mark is her under-standing; yet I would not have you quite drop your reflections on the plainness of her person: for, by continual teazing, you may possibly bring her to say some-thing to the following effect:—That she could not help the plainness of her per-son:—that she endeavoured to be as con-tented as she could; but, in short, she did not much concern herself about the matter.——Then have you a double road for teazing her still more on that head.

If she is clean and well dressed, you

put on a malicious sneer; and, looking her over from top to toe, you may noddle your head; and say, " So, Miss, consi-
" dering you are a Wit, and a lady who
" despises all personal advantages, I must
" needs say you have tricked yourself out
" pretty handsomely to-day." Then may you add, that you would hold a good wager, she was every day longer prinking in the glass than you was.—But it was always so.—You had ever observed, that the ugliest women were much fonder of their persons, than the most beautiful.

If she fails, in the least particular, of nicety in dress, then have you the old beaten path before you: load her with the names of trollop, slattern, slut, dirty beast, &c. omit not any of those trite observations; that all Wits are slatterns;—that no girl ever delighted in reading, that was not a slut;—that well might the men say they would not for the world marry a Wit; and that they had rather have a woman who could make a pudding, than one who could make a poem;—that it was the ruin of all girls who had not independent fortunes, to have learnt either to read or write. You may tell her also, that she may thank God, that her ugliness will preserve her from being a whore.—End all these pious reflections with thanking Heaven, that, for your part, you are no WIT; and that you will take care your children shall not be of that stamp.

To a girl of this sort your fits of kindness must be much more frequent than to any other: for if she has sense, it is ten to one but she will have spirit enough to throw off her chains, if they always appear made of iron: you must therefore gild them over with great real indulgencies; and never let your ill-usage rest long enough upon her mind, to bring her to a proper resolution. Shew also great tenderness and affection to her before company; that if ever she should leave you, she may be generally accused of the highest ingratitude.

I know not whether it would not be best, if the girl has so much spirit, that you are forced to bestow a vast deal of kindness on her, to urge her temper far enough to make her run away. For although it is noble sport to have a girl of sense to work upon, yet it is warm exercise: and, by turning such a one adrift, and taking another of less understanding into your service, you will have a fine opportunity, in all companies, of not only raving at the ingratitude of Miss Fanny, who is gone, but of extolling your own extreme good-nature, in taking Miss Dolly, who is now with you. Besides, you will have some new, pleasant, additional taunts for Miss Dolly: as thus,—If ever you should scold at her, and teaze her enough to make her say the least word in answer, you may say, " Heigh-day! " What!—you too are going to be a girl

" of spirit, are you? I shall hear, I sup-
" pose, that you have taken your flight,
" after the witty Miss Fanny.—But pray
" troop off as soon as you please, Ma-
" dam—I shall not send for you back.—
" But I hope I shall, in time, be convinced
" of my own folly, in thinking there is
" such a thing as gratitude in this world."

Should your humble companion be a
plain girl, with a very moderate degree of
understanding, and great meekness of
temper, you have little to do but to rate
and mortify her continually; only tem-
pering your ill-humour with just kindness
enough to keep her your own. Much
less of that ingredient called kindness
will do in this, than in the two other
cases: for, being sensible of her own defects, such a girl will most likely pine
away her very soul, and lose all her spirit
in grieving at your ill-usage, without
thinking herself capable of any redress,
by leaving you. As soon as she is become

a poor dejected wretch, that trembles at every word you say to her, a little teazing every day will do; and the words Dolt, and Mope, properly applied, will be sufficient. But remember to keep her as much in your sight as possible; because the only chance of comfort she can have, is in being out of your presence.

The foregoing directions are adapted to particular qualifications in your dependent: but I will now add a few general rules, that will be suitable to any girl who is under your command.

Carefully watch in what things your humble companion is most diligent to please you; and be sure never to appear pleased with any such endeavours.

There are some girls so very observant of your commands, and so ready cheerfully to do every thing you desire them, that it is very difficult to catch them at a fault. If you should observe this disposition in Miss Lucy, you may practise a

game which many people, who honour
themselves with the name of humourists,
have played before you : this is, never to
tell any one what you want; but to be
extremely angry, that your servants, your
dependents, and friends, have not the gift
of divination.

Surround yourself with as many peculiarities as you possibly can; and this not
with a design of being pleased (as some
odd people are) with those dependents,
who, observing all such your peculiarities,
hope by that means to please you : but in
order to have more frequent opportunities
of rating your servants, or teazing your
humble companion, as in the following
manner.

Declare, whether true or false, that you
have a great hatred to a noise ; and whenever Miss Lucy steps more softly than
common, in order to please you, tell her,
you wonder how she can stamp about the
floor in such a manner, as if she had

wooden shoes on. Or, if you choose not
to imagine that she stepped loud, then
you may scream out, as soon as she comes
near you, and say, that she has frightened
you out of your wits; for she glided in so
softly, that you took her for a ghost. If
also you observe, that she is uniformly
careful never to offend your ears, by any
noise that she can possibly avoid, you
must never omit saying to her, whenever
she goes out of the room, " Let me *intreat*
" you, child, not to bounce the door after
" you, enough to shake the house." But
you may suffer your own children to make
as much noise as they please, without any
kind of reproof.

If the children, or the servants, make
any complaints against Miss Lucy, be sure
not to hear one word she attempts to say,
in her own defence.

If the complaint comes from your servants, tell her, that you wonder at her
assurance, in speaking to any of your

servants: Or with a sneer, ask her, if she supposes, that you keep servants to wait upon her.

If the complaint against her comes from the children, scold at her (as we say) within an inch of her life. Ask her, how she dares to affront your children? Abuse her, even in the language of Billingsgate, calling her all the scurrilous names you can invent; such as, draggle-tail low-bred creature, scum of the earth, with as many more abusive terms as you can recollect. Then drive her with great impetuosity out of your sight.

These violent 'passions' of scolding I would by no means advise to be too often repeated in this case, any more than to your servants, as they would soon lose their force, and subject you to contempt. But they do extremely well, to come in now-and-then, by way of variety and surprise; especially in this connection, as they are more adapted to frighten half

out of her wits a good-natured inoffensive
girl well-born, and well-bred, than the
lower sort of servants; who, if they should
chance to have been brought up near Billingsgate or St. Giles's, might have been
accustomed to such sort of language.

If your son, Master Jacky, should have
cut Miss Lucy across the face with his
new knife; or your daughter, Miss Isa-
bella, should have pinched her arms black
and blue, or scratched her face and neck,
with her pretty nails, so as to have fetched
the blood; and poor Lucy, to prevent any
farther mischief to her person, should come
and make her complaint to you; do you,
in the first place, rate her soundly for
provoking the poor children, who, you
may affirm, are the best natured little
things in the world, if they are not teazed
and vexed. But if by the blood streaming
from her face or arms, it appears plainly,
that the girl has been very much hurt,
you may (to shew your great impartiality)

say, that you will send for the children in,
and reprimand them. " For it is not my
" way (you may say) to suffer the *lowest*
" creature in my house to be ill-used; nor
" will I, on any account, permit *my* chil-
" dren to behave themselves unbecoming
" their station." Miss Lucy, on this (not
comprehending perhaps the full drift of
your speech), will brighten up a little;
will thank you for your indulgence; and,
if a good-natured girl, will beg you not to
be too severe with master and miss, who,
she hopes, on being spoke to, will do so
no more. Now let your countenance grow
very fierce; ring the bell most furiously;
sternly order the children to be brought
before you; and utter such threats, as will
make poor Miss Lucy tremble for the
consequence, and heartily repent of her
complaint. But how will she be surprised,
if you act this scene well! As soon as
the children come into the room, begin
to rate them most severely.—But for

what?—Why for disobeying your commands, and condescending to play, and be familiar, with any thing but their equals! You may conclude also, by threatening them with the greatest punishment, if ever they are again guilty of so high an offence, as that of speaking to a wretch so much beneath them in birth, fortune, and station, as Miss Lucy.

If you have no children, keep dumb animals enough, and they will pretty near answer all your purposes.

It is not amiss, if your dependent be a girl very apt to blush, to be perpetually, before company, saying things to her, that will keep her in a constant confusion of face, which is as teazing and uneasy a sensation as may be.*

Another pleasant way before company,

* This hint was given me by a female friend, who insisted on my inserting it; although I assured her that the rule was quite needless, as blushing is full as much out of date as high heads.

is, to rail so loudly against laziness, ill-temper, or any other bad quality, that, you may say, *all* girls possess, that your visitors will go away, convinced that poor Lucy is the plague and torment of your life.

If you have chosen a girl (as at first advised) whose parents, when living, were truly kind and indulgent to her, you may amuse yourself with a fine game at compassion with her, as follows:

Begin talking to her of her parents; raise all her tender affections; collect every little circumstance that will awaken her grief, and dissolve her into tears, by painting her loss in the liveliest colours. Carry the scene so far, as to mingle tears with hers; and utter the strongest professions, of being to her, yourself, a second father, mother, friend, and protectress. The poor girl's heart will be almost melted with tender sorrow for the loss of her parents, and with overflowing gratitude to you for your goodness. But, as soon as the latter has, by degrees, begun to over-spread her mind with a joy, that will in a manner dispel her sorrow; can you, my dear pupil, carry this pleasant sport so high, as in that instant to change your kind behaviour? To grow in a rage with her for nothing; and to make the girl more sensible than before of the loss of indulgent parents, by the cruel reverse she now so strongly experiences? If you can do this, you shall have the highest seat in my temple, and I will say,

———— Duris genuit te cautibus horrens
Caucasus, Hyrcanæque admôrunt ubera tigres.
                    VIRG. Æn. l. iv. v. 366.

CHAPTER III.

To Parents.

IT has been said, that the state of children when very young, with regard to their parents, is like the state of a blind man, in the hands of a friend who has the use of his eyes. Children want both protection from harms, and direction in every step they are to take. They are perfectly helpless, and incapable of supporting themselves, even one day, without a parental care over them; and where that care is exerted for their benefit, there they undoubtedly owe the highest duty and regard imaginable.

The most unlimited power was ever given to parents over their children: and in ancient Rome, it was said to extend to life and death. This most probably must arise from a knowledge of the great natural affection and tenderness, that is in almost every living creature towards its offspring; and to such parents as possess this true affection, I direct not my precepts; for where real love and affection towards the children (which must exert itself for their good) is in the heart, all my instructions will be thrown away. But as for you, O ye parents, who are willing to learn, and who intend to make a proper use of your power, let me remind you, that even in this age you are invested, both by law and custom, with the strongest outward and visible power I know of in this land. Purchased slaves are not allowed: your servants if you use them ill may leave you, or can, in many cases, have better redress against you from the magistrate, than you can procure against them. Your children have nobody to fly to, nobody even to complain to! and as it is in your power to take care of these, or cruelly to neglect them; their very lives, whilst infants, are still, in a manner, at your disposal. It is at your own option to feed them on bread and water, the hard fare appointed for criminals, or to pamper them (if you can afford it) with all the dainties of the land. The reins of restraint are yours. The rod of correction is given into your hands: who shall set bounds to your strokes?

These my rules—which positively forbid, not only all manual correction, but every the least degree of restraint or contradiction, to the infant's wayward will, if you intend to breed them up properly, so as to be a torment to themselves if they live, and a plague to all your acquaintance.

Severity to children, when carried to excess, may, indeed, render the lives of those children very miserable; and I allow it to be *one* method of tormenting: but, in my opinion, by no means the best.

Yet, if you intend to follow this method, let me give you one necessary piece of advice; which is, never to strike or whip a child, but when you are angry, and in a violent passion with that child; nor ever let this correction come for lying, obstinacy, or disobedience, in the child, but for having torn or dirted her white frock, if it be a girl; or for having accidentally broke a china cup at play; or any such trifling offence. But there is one strong reason still remains against the least degree of general severity; which is, the regard you ought to have for your own reputation. If your intention be to indulge yourself, without any regard to your child's welfare, why should you take a method by which you may incur the censure of cruelty, when you can more effectually answer your own purpose, and be called kind? Therefore, by all means, humour every child you have to the highest degree, till they attain the age of five or six years; by which time you will be able to judge, whether your indulgence has had a proper effect. If you see them possessed with a due degree of obstinacy, wilfulness, perverseness, and ill-humour; if you find, that the passions of pride, cruelty, malice, and envy, have, like rank weeds, flourished, for want of rooting up, and overwhelmed every spark of goodness in the mind; then may you (as my true disciples) rejoice in having so far done your duty by them, as to have laid the proper foundation for their becoming no small adepts in this our useful science.

If, notwithstanding the uncontrolled licence you have given to your children, of indulging every rising passion, one of them should chance to be endued with such a mildness of disposition, and so much in-bred good-nature, as to have grown up gentle, against your consent; then, to that child, immediately change your method; grow morose and severe;

make favourites of all the rest, and encourage them to teaze and insult it, till you have quite broke its spirit, and got the better of its natural placidness of disposition, so as to turn it into a dejected mope.

But take another view of this extreme indulgence to children; and it is hoped this picture will confirm you in such a practice.

Suppose your stock of children too large; and that, by your care for their support, you should be abridged of some of your own luxuries and pleasures. To make away with the troublesome and expensive brats, I allow, would be the desirable thing: but the question is, how to effect this without subjecting yourself to that punishment which the law has thought proper to affix to such sort of jokes. Whipping and starving, with some caution, might do the business: but, since a late execution for a fact of that kind

may have given a precedent for the ma-
gistrates to examine into such affairs,
you may, by these means, find your way
to the gallows, if you are low enough for
such a scrutiny into your conduct: and,
if you are too high to have your actions
punished, you may possibly be a little ill-
spoken of amongst your acquaintance. I
think, therefore, it is best not to venture,
either your neck, or your reputation, by
such a proceeding; especially as you may
effect the thing, full as well, by following
the directions I have given, of holding no
restraint over them.

Suffer them to climb, without contradiction, to heights from whence they may
break their necks: let them eat every
thing they like, and at all times; not
refusing them the richest meats, and
highest sauces, with as great a variety as
possible; because even excess in one dish
of plain meat cannot, as I have been told
by physicians, do much harm. Suffer

them to sit up as late as they please at
night, and make hearty meat-suppers;
and even in the middle of the night, if
they call for it, do not refuse the poor
things some victuals. By this means, nobody can say you starve your children:
and if they should chance to die of a sur-
feit, or of an ill habit of body, contracted
from such diet, so far will you be from
censure, that your name will be recorded
for a kind and indulgent parent. If any
impertinent person should hint to you,
that this manner of feeding your children
was the high road to their destruction,
you may answer, " That the poor people
" suffer their children to eat and drink
" what they please, not feeding them
" upon bread-pudding, milk and water,
" and such stuff, as the physicians advise;
" and (you may say) where do you see
" any thing more healthful, than the
" children of the poor?" Take my word
for it, you may make this appeal without

fear of contradiction; for often have I heard it made in company, and never yet did I hear it observed, that the poor, in truth, had not the hurtful things to give their children, which it is in the power of the rich to indulge them in; that the food of these healthy poor children generally is bread-and-cheese, plain bread, a little fat bacon, clear water, or some small-beer, hardly removed one degree from water itself; and not roast-meat, fish, hashes, soups, &c. &c. But to return to my farther directions.

On no account miss that useful season of the year, the summer; in which you may give your children as much fruit as they can cram down their throats: then be sure not to contradict the poor little things, if they should choose to play about, and overheat themselves, in the middle of the day; and afterwards should choose to cool their limbs, by sprawling about on the wet grass, after the dew is fallen. If they should chance, after all this, to outlive the month of September, without the worms, a fever, the small-pox, or a general corruption of blood, that no medicine can purify, you must wait the event of another summer. From having indulged them in all their humours, you have one chance more of losing them in sickness than those parents have, who control them; which is, that it is not (you know) in the power of medicine to cure, when it is not in your power to get that medicine down the child's throat. On all considerations, therefore, I believe, we may venture to affirm, that letting children entirely alone to their own wills, without the least degree of restraint or contradiction, is the surest road to lead them to their own destruction.

If parents, in the foregoing process, should be able, with truth, to deny the motive I have assigned, can they, with equal truth, deny the probable

consequence, here shewn, of such indulgence?

Supposing your child, or children, to
outlive all these your kind indulgences,
encourage them in all sorts of cruelty;
first to flies and birds, then to dogs, cats,
or any other animals, that come in their
way. This will habituate them to that
true hardness of heart, which is the
foundation of our science.

So pleasant is the sport of tormenting
domestic animals under our protection,
that a whole chapter of instructions for
that purpose should have been inserted,
had it not been already very well exemplified in Pompey the Little.* And if
my readers have the gift of imitation, they
may, by many pleasant examples, become
perfect in this practice.

Although I would have you inculcate
the love of cruelty, yet, by no means, call
it by its true name; but encourage them

* Book i. chap. 9.

G

in the practice of it under the name of
FUN. When they are well versed in this
sport of tormenting amongst animals,
they may introduce it, under the aforesaid
name, amongst their friends and acquaintance. It will equally answer in all
stations; for how many hurt shins, bloody
noses, broken heads, if not broken bones,
has this sport caused at a country wake?
and, in politer life, how many heavy hearts
have retired from company, by the means
of joke, repartee, and FUN?

And that this kind of FUN is allowed
to be extremely diverting, appears from
its being so very common to hear people
publicly declare, that they always laugh
at mischief.

If your children happen to have but
weak understandings, upbraid them with
every excellence you see abroad; and
lament your own hard fate in being
plagued with idiots. But,

If you see a rising genius in any child

(especially if it be a girl), unless you can in some way turn it to your own profit, give that child no assistance nor encouragement; but browbeat all endeavours towards striking out of the common road.

When once your children are grown up to men or women's estate, let the very appearance of indulgence vanish; and, as soon as they are come to a relish of this world's enjoyment, restrain them with a heavy hand. Upbraid them, also, with your former kindness; lament that your past indulgence to them, when children, has made them ungrateful; and declare them to be the grief and torment of your old age.

As you never contradicted or rebuked them, when children, remember that you have in store a large quantity of contradiction and rebukes at their service; of both which be as lavish as possible, particularly of the latter, which will now be of no sort of service; especially if you

bestow such rebukes on them before company, and in the roughest terms.

Study the tempers of your sons and
daughters, to see what they most delight
in; and, as you have an absolute restrain-
ing power, exercise it where it will be
most strongly felt.

If gaiety and public diversion are their
delight, confine them constantly at home;
or let them out with such restrictions as
will damp all their joy. But if they have
no immoderate love for such amusement,
and could be as well contented at home,
from the satisfaction they would take in
doing their duty, let your chief point be
to dress them out, and send them abroad,
for your own honour and credit; and
receive them with ill-humour when they
come home. If their chief joy be in endeavouring, by their cheerful conversation,
to please and amuse you, put on such a
rigid austerity, as shall make them afraid
to open their lips before you; and with-

hold from them the least appearance of pleasure or good-humour in yourself, for their readiness in all things to comply with your will.

Spare no expence in dress or equipage for them, provided their dispositions are such, that it will give them no pleasure: for how must an old Harlowe enjoy himself in loading a Clarissa with money, clothes, jewels, &c. whilst he knows, that all she wants from him, is kind looks and kind words!

When your daughter comes to be old enough to marry, if she should happen to have fixed her affections on a real deserving young man, and you should be bent upon her giving her hand to one whose only merit is his riches, the behaviour of old Western to his daughter Sophia, in Tom Jones, will shew you how a fond father should treat a deserving child.

There is more difficulty in giving positive rules for the tormenting children, than

any other connection whatever; as my
pupils must have two points to carry:
one is, the child's own discomfort; and
the other is, the use they are of in tormenting all your friends and acquaintance. Should you follow the road of those
parents, who hold a proper restraint, and
keep a watchful eye, over their children,
in order to prevent their hurting themselves; should you make that parent your
example, who, by carefully watching every
rising passion, accustoms the child (if not
to subdue) at least to keep it within proper bounds; should you act in the manner
of those parents, who, by cultivating and
encouraging every good disposition in
their children, breed them up with mo-
desty and gentleness of mind; and who,
by well-placed kindness and REAL indulgence, have inspired them with a grateful
and affectionate regard towards themselves; children thus educated would, I
confess, when grown up, in all probability,

be more fitted to receive your torments, than those bred up by my rules. But many contingencies might then arise to prevent the exercise of your power: as your own death, your son's going out in the world, or your daughter's marriage. I give it once more, therefore, as my advice, that you should leave such kind of education for those who have no relish for our sport; and that you pursue the method called INDULGENCE, which I have already marked out. This will infallibly make them miserable while infants; as common experience must shew you, that no children are so fretful, peevish, and uneasy, as those who are so indulged. And although you may, by this means, breed up a parcel of head-strong, hard-hearted cubs, who, when old enough, will defy your power; yet you may, in the mean time, amuse yourself with your servants, your acquaintance, and your friends, who may chance to be more fitted by nature, or education, for your purpose. You may go out of the world, also, with the pleasing reflection, that you have left behind you a set of wolves, cats, and foxes, of your own educating; who will help to plague and torment all the rest of mankind.

The reason there is no chapter of instructions to children, how to plague their parents, we presume, is pretty obvious. First, because when they are very young, they cannot read. It lies, therefore, upon you, O ye parents! to make them, in their infancy, both a plague to themselves, and all around them. In the next place, when they are grown old enough to profit by my instructions, they may find, in some of the succeeding chapters, most of the rules that could possibly be given them: which, it is hoped, they will be so kind as to practise on all those parents, who, by departing from my institutes, have given their children an affection-power over them: for such power will the children gain, if you turn your parental authority into an affectionate friendship towards them.

Could I be so happy as to prevail with you to follow my directions, no other instructions would hereafter be necessary. For ye must be sensible, O ye parents! how much it is in your power to form the minds of your children so as to enrol them under my list, or to guard their tender minds against my precepts, if Solomon was in the right when he said, *Train up your child, &c.*

CHAPTER IV.

To the Husband.

The visible power of the husband comes next to that of the parent: for I think it has been determined in our public courts of justice, by some unpolite professors of the law, that a husband may exercise his marital authority so far, as to give his wife moderate correction.

How happy is it for English wives, that the force of custom is so much stronger than our laws! How fortunate for them, that the men, either through affection or indolence, have given up their legal rights; and have, by custom, placed all the power in the wife!

Mistake me not so much, as to think, that I intend to assert, there are no tyrannical or bad husbands; daily experience would soon contradict such an assertion. But the sport of tormenting is not the husband's chief game. If he grows indifferent to his wife, or comes to hate her, he wishes her dead, or absent; and therefore, if in low life, often takes such violent measures, as to break her bones, or to break her heart: and if in high life, he keeps mistresses abroad, and troubles not his head, one way or other, about his wife.

But there are a set of men in a middle station, who cannot, on account of their fortunes, or reputation, well follow either of the above-mentioned methods: and to such (if there are any amongst them who are governed by their wives) I address this chapter; and hope to hit off a few strokes that may be fit for their practice.

It has been already endeavoured to be shewn, in what manner a patroness may plague an humble companion; but in the married state, it has, sometimes, been the practice of the husband, to take into his house (I will not say into his bed) a female *humble* companion to torment his wife. If he chooses this method of proceeding, let him select a handsome vixen; and there are, I believe, few female spirits, who will accept of such an office, but, without the help of my precepts, will thoroughly answer the husband's purpose in that situation, of plaguing, vexing, and insulting his wife, as much as he can possibly desire.

My rules (as before observed) will in this connection be 'of little use in high life, as it is seldom the concern amongst the great (with some few exceptions) either to please or plague each other: but, in a more moderate degree, husbands may proceed in the following manner.

The best foundation to work on, is to be sure to mistake your wife's character; praise her for what she does not deserve, and overlook every good quality she is in reality possessed of. As it is a very common practice, for women to pretend a dislike to smoaking, only because their husbands are fond of it, so do you take care to observe, whether your wife likes or dislikes tobacco: if the smoke of it should really make her sick, which is sometimes the case, be sure never to be without a pipe in your mouth, and rail most heartily, at the affectation of ALL wives, who pretend not to love the smell of tobacco. Never let the time of dinner pass, without being displeased with every thing that comes to the table. You may blame your wife for the fault of the fish-monger, the poulterer, the butcher, and the cook; particularly the latter, as it gives an ill-natured wench (who hears from the footman this your kind and tender practice) an opportunity of wreaking her spleen on her mistress, by the wrong-headed anger of her master.

Give the highest commendations to

every thing you meet with abroad; and if your wife, thinking to please you, should provide the same things for you at home, be doubly displeased with such things; and declare, that the reason you are so much abroad, and spend so much time in a tavern, is, that by the negligence of your wife you are half-starved at your own table.

If you have a very careful prudent wife, one, who by her good œconomy confines all the expenses under her inspection fairly within her appointment, part with your money to her, like so many drops of your blood; and read her a lecture on extravagance, for every necessary that is bought into the house; at the same time sparing no expense for your own hounds, horses, or claret, to treat your brother sportsmen.

Should you have been abroad for the whole, or any part of the day, be sure to come home in an exceeding ill-humour, if you have a wife at home who knows how to value your good humour. The more cheerfully she receives you, the more sour and morose do you grow upon the same: or, if you choose not to carry the joke so high, a sullen discontent, with several yawns expressive of indifference, if not dislike, to your own home, will do very well. Besides, for this latter behaviour, nobody can blame you, as it will (by custom) be set down to the account of low spirits, or some violent fatigue you may have undergone. It has been observed, that more fidelity is often found in the bad part of mankind to the bad, than in the good to the good. It is also, I believe, as true, that much more tenderness and indulgence is generally exerted towards the counterfeits of any weakness or distress, than to those who labour under a real weakness of body, or affliction of mind. These are facts; let the searchers into human nature declare their causes.

But in this wilful want of distinguishing, lies the chief power of tormenting. If polygamy was allowed, greatly could this chapter be enlarged; for fine sport might a man have among many wives, by confounding their characters, being fond of the bad, being cruel to the good, with several other very pleasant amusements. And that some husbands have a good notion of this kind of diversion, we may, I think, fairly infer from what we now see, with regard to those who have had two, three, or four wives in succession. For, if ever you hear, that a man has made an exceeding good husband to one wife, and an exceeding bad husband to another, let the matter be examined into, and it will generally be found, that his indulgence and fondness were placed on an high-spirited vixen, or a wayward insipid doll; whilst his neglect, his ill-humour, and his cruelty, were all bestowed on a meek-spirited wife, whose affection and regard for him made her deserve better treatment. Yet still, as things are now circumstanced, my rules for the husband can be but few. However, should a man happen to have a very deserving woman for his wife, I think I can recommend this our art to him, as productive of some diversion. But as his power would then arise, not from his exterior authority, but from the affection of his wife; I must still beg the favour of all those husbands, who intend to study this science, that they would collect rules for themselves, from any of the chapters that may hit their case, in my Second Division.

ESSAY

ON THE

ART OF TORMENTING.

PART II.

PART II.

THIS Second part is addressed to those, who have no legal exterior authority, but who may be said to have an interior power arising from the affection of the person, with whom they are connected. This power, if properly used for the torment of those, whose affections you have gained, will be found strong enough greatly to overbalance any exterior power; and is indeed so effectual for the purpose I recommend, that in the case of the husband no one carried this sport very far, but by dropping his marital authority, and teazing his wife through her real love and regard for him.

A few of the connections only are taken in this Second Division; and we will begin with that of the lover, as in the following chapter.

CHAPTER I.

To Lovers.

THIS connection gives so large a field for the exercise of our pleasant art, that it cannot be passed over in silence: yet very short will be this chapter; for does any one want directions in what he is already perfect? Who is there that cannot, without my help, carry his food to his mouth, or perform the office of respiration? Teazing and tormenting is the sustenance, the breath, the very life, of most young women who are sure of the affections of their lovers. Nor are the men less expert at the practice of teazing, when they know themselves to be the objects of a woman's love.

Give me leave, therefore, only to pay my compliments to these my best adepts;

begging, that the ladies, if they find their
memory or invention at a loss for a true
coquette-behaviour, would read over most
of our comedies since the Restoration;
and that they would not fail to make the
favourite characters of such comedies their
exemplars.

CHAPTER II.

To the Wife.

THE common disposition with which a married couple generally come together (except for mere lucrative motives) is this.

The man, for some qualification, either personal or mental, which he sees,* or dreams he sees, in some woman, fixes his affections on that woman; then, instead of endeavouring to fix her affections on himself, he directs all her thoughts, and her enjoyment, on settlements, equipage, fine cloaths, and every other gratification of vanity within his power and fortune to give her. He pays so thorough an adoration and submission to her in all respects;

---

* Aut videt, aut vidisse putat——
VIRG. Lib. vi. v. 454.

that he soon perfects a work, perhaps,
before, half finished to his hands, namely,
the making her completely and immovably
in love with—herself.—This puts her, for
the present, into such good spirits, and
good-humour, that the poor man, from
the pleasure he finds in her company, be-
lieves her to be in love with him. This
thought, joined to his first inclination to
her person, creates in him a pretty strong
affection towards her, and gives her that
power over him, which I would willingly
assist her in exerting. This affection, when
he becomes her husband, generally shews
itself in real kindness. But as soon as all
the joy arising from courtship is gone, the
wife generally grows uneasy; her husband,
being no longer her lover, grows disgustful to her; and, if she be a woman of
violent passions, she turns fractious and
sour; and a breach soon ensues. The
husband may bluster, and rave, and talk
of his authority and power, as much as

he pleases; but it is very easy to grow
into such a perfect disregard of such
storms, that, by wrapping one's self up in
a proper degree of contempt, they will
blow as vainly over our heads, as the wind
over our houses. Besides, if there are not
emoluments enough in the husband's
house, to make it worth while to bear the
ill-humours raised by our own frowardness,
separation is the word; to which if a husband will not consent, a cause of cruelty
against him, in Doctors Commons, will
soon bring him to; for (as I have heard)
the husband there, by paying the expenses
of both sides, will be obliged, in a manner,
to supply his wife with the means of carrying her own point, and will be glad therefore to make any conditions with her.
But a woman of prudence will know
when she is well; will take no such pre-
cipitate steps; but will rejoice in the discovery of her husband's great affection
towards her, as a means for pursuing the

course of teazing and tormenting, which I here recommend,

··Oh the joy it is to have a good servant, cried Sophronia, who had not goodness of heart enough to be kind to any human creature, and whose joy must therefore arise from having a proper subject to torment! But with what ecstasy then might the artful Livia cry out—Oh the joy it is to have a good husband!

If you bring a large fortune to your husband, custom and example will justify you in being as insolent as you please. Solomon himself bears testimony to the intolerable yoke a man takes upon his neck, who submits to be supported by his wife. But my advice is, that if you bring no fortune to your husband, you should be as insolent as if you had increased his store by thousands. This, I own, is a bold stroke; but does not want its precedents. If a man marries you without a fortune, and raises you, perhaps, many degrees

from the state to which you was born, is
it not for his honour, that you should shew
him that your spirit can rise with your
fortune? In what can a woman shew her
spirit more, than in insolence and opposition? for are ye not taught from your
cradles, that submission and acquiescence
is *meanness*, and unbecoming a woman of
spirit? Not but you may insult your husband frequently with the words duty and
obedience, provided you never are *mean*
enough to bring them into your practice.
If the fortune (as before observed) be entirely on your husband's side, you may
also be pretty sure of the strength of his
affection towards you, as that alone could
determine his choice; and therefore you
have the firmest foundation to work upon.
There is, besides, another deep malignant
pleasure, that must arise in the breast of
every woman, that makes a vexatious and
tormenting wife, to a man who has gene-
rously lifted her from distress and obscurity

into affluence and splendor; I mean, the hope that her example will deter many a man from conferring the like obligation. This, I confess, may save some men from being plagued with a termagant; but I rather believe, that it will prevent many a good girl's happiness; as also the happiness of every generous man, who is thus scared from attempting the likeliest method (if there be such a thing as gratitude in a female breast) for conjugal felicity.

If your husband is not a man of an independent fortune, but is in any trade or profession; if also he should have met with misfortunes and rubs enough to have kept him back from the high road to riches, be sure to shew such a despondency towards every scheme or step he takes for the advancement of his fortune, as will sink and depress his spirits, and render him fearful of the event of almost every undertaking. Add also your earnest advice against every proposal he makes. By this means, you will hang such a weight on him, that he will have no enjoyment of his life. Should his schemes and endeavours succeed, you may enjoy the fruits of his industry, and find other ways enough to plague him; but should they fail, let him not want the additional load of your reproaches for not having followed your advice; and you may lament as loudly as you please, for your poor self, and your poor children. Say boldly to him, " See, " barbarous man, how, by your miscon- " duct, you have ruined my children." For you must seem absolutely to forget, that your husband has any share in your mutual offspring, although you see him pierced with the most poignant affliction by his fears for their future welfare. And in this, Custom will countenance you enough to take off all fear of censure from the world for such a practice.

If you marry a widower with children,

I would rather advise you to consider those children as a means put into your hands to plague your husband, than as new subjects for you to torment.

If you yourself are a widow, the well known path lies before you, of insulting, plaguing, and tormenting your second husband by praises of your first. And this practice is so well established, that we have an old law, which advises no man to marry a widow, unless her first husband was hanged.

A woman, by her profligate behaviour, may bring infamy on herself and her husband: by her extravagance, she may attempt to ruin him: or by a violent termagancy of temper, she may never suffer him to have a moment's peace or quiet in his house. But these enormities, it is presumed, will render her detestable in the eyes of the world, and may put her husband on some measures of redress. Her extravagance with some difficulty may be restrained; for her scandalous intrigues, a divorce from her may be obtained; and if a man finds perpetual storms and ill-humour at home, he is at liberty to fly from so hateful a place. Such violent measures therefore, as I have the highest regard to the reputation of my pupils, I absolutely forbid. It is your delicate strokes I recommend, and those must come from pretended fondness.

You may complain of every hour your husband spends from you with any of his friends, as robbing you of his dear company. You may frequently repeat the following fond speech mentioned in the Spectator, " You are all the world to me; " and why should not I be all the world " to you?"

Be sure not to like or approve of any of your husband's friends; and, when in company with them, say so many half-rude things, as will keep him in a continual fright for you; and will make him hasten

I

them away as soon after dinner as possible, to prevent your exposing yourself; and, perhaps, exposing him to a quarrel, in order to support your ill-manners. As soon as your husband returns home, you may fall on his friends for taking him away from you; and abuse them with all the virulence you are mistress of. But should you have indulged yourself in railing at them, and have said so many bitter things against them, as to have grated your husband's soul, and to have raised in him a little degree of anger, you have nothing to do but to own yourself a weak, silly, fond woman, apt, you may confess, to take prejudices, nay, aversions, to those who would endeavour to share with you the least portion of your husband's affections. Then, bursting into tears, you may add, that nothing but the most hardhearted wretch in the world could be angry with his poor wife, for hating any body out of love to him; but you *did* and *would* hate and detest them all, as long as you lived. On this your husband will be forced to sue for reconcilement; which you must by no means grant, till you have brought him to acknowledge, that the highest mark of affection you can shew towards him, is to hate and abhor all those whom he esteems and loves. This behaviour, even towards his men friends, will pass for love; but, as to all his female acquaintance, you need not fear shewing the highest degree of jealousy towards every woman he speaks to: nay, you may, to shew your extravagant fondness for him, watch his very eyes in company, and fail not to upbraid him with unkindness, for looking at any woman besides yourself. Let a smart curtain lecture also be the certain consequence of his having spoke, with the least degree of praise or approbation, of any woman whatsoever. These practices must be where you know they will teaze, and

where, also, you have not any real cause
for jealousy. But should you have reason
to think, that your husband is false to
you, it is a very nice point: I have heard
of wives, who, by a seeming blindness to
their husbands inconstancy, and by a
double portion of cheerfulness and good-
humour, have recalled their wandering
affections: the husband also, by this amiable behaviour in his wife, like a man near
shipwrecked in the stormy seas, has been
so enamoured of his native home, as never
more to quit so happy an asylum as the
kind bosom of such a wife. This method,
it is true, recalls the husband (if he is worth
recalling;) but it makes him blest; and is,
therefore, unfit for the practice of my
pupils. The man in our case, likewise,
if possible, must be recalled, and got into
trammels; for which reason, open rage
and resentment against him for his inconstancy must be suppressed, as it might
drive him from the company of his cross

wife to the arms of his kind mistress.
However, I think you may venture to
throw forth as much rage and venom as
you please against the hated strumpet
who has deprived you of your lawful property. You may excuse your husband,
by inveighing against the cunning arts of
bad women, who make it their business to
draw aside easy-tempered, unwary men.
You may declare your fondness so great
for dear Billy, that you can forgive *him*
any thing, although you are determined,
if possible, to stab or poison the base
wanton harlot who seduced him from your
lawful bed : then, casting your fond arms
about his neck, you may utter such a mix-
ture of feigned love, and real reproaches,
as will entangle him too strongly to make
him break from you, and yet will make
him wish himself surrounded with a swarm
of hornets, rather than encircled with such
tormenting endearments.

If your husband has sisters, and is fond

of them, study every art of behaviour
towards them, that will plague and vex
him. Be sometimes over-civil and formal
to them; at other times perfectly rude,
insolent, and ill-bred: but never leave, till
you have, by some means or other, entirely
alienated your husband's affections from
them. Then change your views, and consider *them* as new subjects of your own
power; practise every art of teazing and
tormenting towards them; and your husband also (if he is under proper management, and you have a due influence over
him) will join with you in the sport: and
unless they, by some means of independ-
ence, escape your power, you cannot well
have better game.

When a man has married a real gentle-
spirited, good woman, I have sometimes
seen the husband's sisters attempting this
sort of pastime with her, but, generally,
with very ill success; unless the husband
be of so mighty uncommon a temper, as

to suffer any woman, who is *not* his bed-fellow, to have the least ascendency over him: but these cases are so very rare, that I cannot help advising my pupils, whose brothers are married, not to shew their teeth, where they are so little likely to bite; but rather to wait, till they themselves can be so happy as to get a man on their side, who will support them in all their tricks and insolence.

Besides nourishing in your mind an inveterate hatred against all your husband's relations and acquaintance, you may shew the highest dislike to every place he was fond of before he married: but express the highest joy and raptures on the very mention of any place, that you used to live in yourself before you was married; and be as lavish as possible of your praises of a single life. You may also, if your husband be not of a very jealous temper, hoard up a parcel of favourite trinkets, as rings, snuff-boxes, &c. which were given you before marriage; and let it appear, from your immoderate fondness for those baubles, that the givers of them are still nearest to your heart.

Carefully study your husband's temper, and find out what he likes, in order never to do any one thing that will please him.

If he expresses his approbation of the domestic qualities of a wife; such as family œconomy, and that old-fashioned female employment, the needle; neglect your family as much as ever his temper will bear; and always have your white gloves on your hands. Tell him, that every woman of spirit ought to hate and despise a man who could insist on his wife's being a family drudge; and declare, that you will not submit to be a cook and a sempstress to any man. But if he loves company, and cheerful parties of pleasure, and would willingly have you always with him, nose him with your great love of needle-work and housewifery. Or should he be a man of genius, and should employ his leisure hours in writing, be sure to shew a tasteless indifference to every thing he shews you of his own. The same indifference, also, may you put on, if he should be a man who loves reading, and is of so communicative a disposition, as to take delight in reading to you any of our best and most entertaining authors. If, for instance, he desires you to hear one of Shakspeare's plays, you may give him perpetual interruptions, by sometimes going out of the room, sometimes ringing the bell to give orders for what cannot be wanted till the next day; at other times taking notice (if your children are in the room), that Molly's cap is awry, or that Jackey looks pale; and then begin questioning the child, whether he has done any thing to make himself sick. If you have needle-work in your hands, you may be so busy in cutting out, and measuring one part with another, that it will plainly appear to your husband, that you mind not one word he reads. If all this teazes him enough to make him call on you for your attention, you may say, that indeed you have other things to mind besides poetry; and if he was uneasy at your taking care of your family and children, and mending *his* shirts, you wished he had a learned wife; and then he would soon see himself in a gaol, and his family in rags. Fail not to be as eloquent as possible on this subject; for I could bring you numberless precedents of silly and illiterate wives, who have half talked their husbands to death, in exclaiming against the loquacity of ALL women, who have any share of understanding or knowledge.

If your husband should be a musical man, you will have many opportunities of teazing and plaguing him. Frequent interruptions and noises, by yourself or children, may be played off upon him; and you must take such an aversion to the sound of all musical instruments, and to all the tribe of fiddlers (as you may call them), that your husband, wearied out by your clamour, may, possibly, give up his favourite amusement. But should you not have power enough over him to carry your point in that manner, you have nothing for it but the old trick of indifference, and sullen dislike, both to his own performance in music, and to any collection of hands by which he might hope to give you some entertainment. Be out of humour when your husband brings company home: be angry, if he goes abroad without you; and troublesome, if he takes you with him.

If your husband be a real domestic man; if he takes delight in his own family, and the company of his wife and children; then be sure never to be easy in your own house; but let visiting, plays, operas, Vauxhall, Ranelagh, &c. be your chief delight. The least restraint from any of these gives you a fair opportunity for pouts or wrangling; and you will also have the whole sex on your side, against the barbarous man who should deny his poor wife the free enjoyment of such innocent amusements.

If your husband should be willing either to stay at home, to go abroad, or to lead any kind of life that would be most agreeable to you, never let him find out what *would* be most agreeable to you: this may be done either by a childish pettishness, and wayward ill-humour with every thing he proposes, or by a mock compliance: for when he says, " Would you like, my " dear, to do so, or so ?" you may answer, " Let it be just what you like, Mr. B—; " for you know I never dispute your will."

If your husband, on observing you particularly fond of something at a friend's table, should desire you to get it for yourself at home, you may say, that you are so little selfish, that you cannot bear to provide any thing for your own eating; and this you may boldly declare, although it should be your common practice to provide some delicacy for yourself every day. It is most likely, that your husband will let this pass; but if he should not, you may, on detection, fly to tears, and complaints of his cruelty and barbarity, in upbraiding you with so small an indulgence as that of a chicken, or a tart, sometimes, for your own eating, when he knows, that your weak stomach will not give you leave to make the horselike meals that he does.

If you manage this scene rightly, and sufficiently reiterate in your husband's ears the words cruel, unkind, barbarous, &c. he will, it is most likely, forget the true occasion of all this uproar; will begin to think he had been a little hard upon you in taking notice of a daily indulgence, which he himself had not only allowed, but requested you to accept; he will ask your pardon, and confess himself in fault, doubling his diligence for the future, in providing all sorts of rarities to gratify your palate.

Be it observed, that this knack of turning the tables, and forcing the offended person to ask pardon of the first aggressor, is one of the most ingenious strokes of our art; and may be practised in every connection, where the power is founded in love.

But to return:

Should your husband, instead of desiring you to please yourself, provide something for you without your knowlege (as many kind husbands have done) in order to give you a small unexpected pleasure, then be sure not to touch a mouthful of it; and, if your circumstances are but low, you may upbraid him with his extravagance for buying what he can so little afford.

This cannot easily be practised in high life, where all sorts of elegancies and rarities are every day provided; but still, if you have a fond husband, you may, in the midst of the highest plenty, give him no small uneasiness, even in this article of eating, by never letting him see you swallow half enough, to keep body and soul together. But do not mistake me in this point, and really starve yourself to vex your husband: for if you have a trusty Abigail, she will daily bring you up, into your own dressing-room, a boiled chicken, a roasted sweetbread, or any other thing you like; and there are ways enough from your own private purse to bribe her to secrecy.

When your husband is absent, insist so strongly on a letter from him every post, that he shall often be put to the highest inconvenience to write, or will suffer great uneasiness from the thought of your being disappointed. The very first time you receive not the expected letter, make no allowances for the carelessness of servants,

who carry letters to the post-house, or for
twenty trifling incidents that may be the
cause of your disappointment; but *say*
that you are sure some dreadful accident
has happened. Then immediately hire a
man and horse, and send him, if it be
two hundred miles, to enquire after your
dear husband's health; or you may get
into a post-chaise, and go yourself. But
should your worldly circumstances be
such, as not to be in the least hurt by this
expensive messenger; or should your husband be so situated, that your coming to him
would be neither very perplexing or inconvenient, then hire no such messenger;
take no such journey; but stay and enjoy
yourself in the place you are in; only fail
not to write to him such a letter, as will
heartily vex him, and keep him upon the
fret, with the thoughts of your uneasiness
(whilst you are very cheerful and merry)
till a post or two will clear up the matter to
him, and he, poor man, is at last satisfied,

that you are no longer miserable with your fears for his health and safety.

This practice of letter-writing, if properly managed, is one of the most fruitful branches of our trade; but seems too well known, to need more than this short hint upon that subject.

When your husband is from home (but not far distant), although you should be in ever so good health, in ever so high spirits, and should be enjoying yourself, in his absence, with a set of your own friends and acquaintance; yet the very instant he appears, throw a languidness into your countenance; let your voice grow small; complain of every ailment incident to the human body; and appear so perfectly dejected and low-spirited, that your fond husband will be under the utmost anxiety about you. Instead of finding his own house the seat of joy and gladness, and meeting with a cheerful companion there, to heighten his

K

pleasures, and alleviate his cares, he will
find his own spirits depressed; he will be
obliged to stifle every cheerful incident
he might have collected for your amusement; he must either give himself up to
melancholy and discomfort at home (for
your friends, if he stayed, would, on seeing the part you intended to act, soon
troop off), or he must seek relief by flight,
and associating with his companions
abroad. Should the latter be his choice,
then the day is your own. You may, the
moment his back is turned, resume your
spirits, your good-humour, your gaiety,
and make merry with your friends. You
need not blush for the appearance this
will make to THEM; for if your visitors
are married females, it is ten to one, but
they have, some of them, often practised
the same themselves. Nor need you be
apprehensive of the others for telling tales
upon you; even although they should
detest your odious pranks: for out of the

many hundred (I will not say thousand) husbands, that have been served this trick, I ask if one single one was ever yet informed of this kind of pleasant behaviour in his wife?

CHAPTER III.

To the Friend.

Before I begin my instructions on this head, it is necessary to say something concerning the article of friendship itself, of which, I think, there are to be found three several sorts.

An ingenious French writer has indeed divided them into many more; but as they all (except one) come under my second or third head, I shall not in this place follow his division.

The first sort is that real, true, and reciprocal friendship, which was said to subsist between Pylades and Orestes, Castor and Pollux, and between several others, that are to be found in certain books——and perhaps no-where else——

The second is that sort of intercourse,

where good-fellowship, good wine, and a certain sympathetical idleness, draw people together; and in such a society, till they quarrel about some trifle or other, they generally choose to call one another by the name of FRIEND.

The third sort is where one person has a real capacity for the exercise of such friendship, as was shewn from Jonathan to David; and who from a desire of energizing this his favourite affection, has attached himself to an artful cunning man.

It is in this third class alone, that my rules can properly be exercised. To all those therefore, who, by the specious bait of pretended goodness and benevolence, have been so lucky as to have drawn on upon their hook one of those gudgeons, I shall address the instructions in this chapter.

In the first place, be very careful not to mistake your man. The marks by which you may know your proper dupes are as follow:

An honest, open countenance is a very good sign: for there is much more in physiognomy, than people generally seem to allow.

If he talks in company greatly in praise of benevolence, good-nature, generosity, charity, &c. hold yourself in some doubt of him: but if his praises of the above virtues seldom flow from his mouth, except to commend some living person, who has done a humane or generous action, you may make a farther trial of him. However, don't thoroughly trust him (for all his fine talking), till you can catch him doing such actions himself, as far as is within his power; doing them, also, without ostentation. Then mark him down as your own; and you may make good sport with him, if you rightly understand the game.

There is one mistake which people have often run into, in their choice of a dupe; namely, in thinking, that the principal qualification to be insisted on is, his having a soft place in his head; whereas the chief thing to seek after is, the man who has a soft place in his heart. Many a disappointment has arose, from fixing your choice on a fool; for frequently will you find such a want of affection, such a thorough selfishness, so much cunning and obstinacy, annexed to folly, that all your labour will be thrown away.

The interested use that is to be made of your friends, I shall not here enlarge upon, as there are so many good examples already published, to which I could refer my reader for his practice on that head; particularly the behaviour of Jonathan Wild * towards his friend Mr. Heartfree. Besides, in this practice, you can give but one heavy blow; nor is there much scope for continual teazing and tormenting, as it is the nature of these generous dupes, while you are ruining them, to be pleased

* Life of Jonathan Wild.

and delighted with their power of serving you. When you have, indeed, entirely ruined them, and openly laugh at them for their silly credulity, they will, on the discovery of your baseness, feel, at first, a sudden shock, with a sort of rent in their affectionate hearts, for being forced to change friendly love and confidence into distrust and abhorrence: but this, in a gentle mind, will soon subside into resignation (and even compassion to you, for the wretched state of wickedness you are in); and it will never more be in your power to deceive or vex them.

The common practice of deserting their friends in distress, men who choose such a proceeding, are already too well versed in to need my instructions. It is not your obvious or trite practices, but your more refined strokes, that I would wish to point out. There is also another objection to the absolutely deserting your friends in distress of circumstances; which is as follows: the only pleasure you can propose (you know) from such desertion, is, that your friend may be starved, or reduced to a very abject state: now, in all probability, you will be deceived in your hope; for when people's nearest and best friends desert them, it is very common for them to find assistance from strangers, where they least expected it. Nay, there are some strange people, so bent upon defeating the purposes of ungenerous friends or relations, that they will, underhand, without desiring any acknowledgments, without so much as putting it in the power of the obliged to make them any return, send handsome presents to those who want: nor will they give you any clue to guess from whence such bounty comes, unless you happen to know their disposition to be so noble, and generous, that you cannot be at a loss to know where your real and grateful thanks are due. Besides, another strong reason against the absolute desertion of your friends, is, that it might make you ill spoken of amongst those who have no notion of any pleasure higher, than that of relieving their friend's distress. I would rather, therefore, advise a method, which would answer the purpose of tormenting much better; and would, at the same time, gain you the reputation of generosity amongst all those who enquire not beyond the outward appearance of any one's actions.

If your friend should come to any worldly misfortune, be sure, in the first place, not to fail telling him (and that repeatedly), that it was entirely by his own fault. Then add as many aggravating speeches as you can heap together. Be very lavish to him of your advice to do impossibilities ;* but stir not a step for his relief, except he should be so nearly connected to you in blood, that your

* See Mr. Orgueil to David Simple, Vol. last. Book vi. Chap. 4.

reputation, as before observed, will suffer by such a total neglect. In that case, you may either take him into your house (if he will come thither); and let him, according to the old saying, live the life of a toad under a harrow; or make him some shabby allowance,* hardly enough to keep him from starving, but sufficient to prevent his seeking for support from any other means, without risking your displeasure, for not resting satisfied with what you thought a sufficient subsistence.

As I have the highest regard for the reputation of my pupils, I would, if possible, form all my instructions upon that plan; and have endeavoured, to the utmost, to follow the exemplars they are taken from; who are not the openly cruel and hardhearted, but rather the specious pretenders to goodness, who, under an outcry about

---

* This exemplified by the author of David Simple, in Familiar Letters, Vol. i. Let. 5. Vol. ii. Let. 21.

benevolence, hide the most malevolent hearts.

If your own affluence, and your friend's indigence, should ever put it in your power to practise the above rule, it will be as effectual for tormenting, as any in this collection; not from the obvious reason of your friend's being near starving, or his wanting the necessaries of life; for those inconveniences are trifling, in comparison with the pain and anguish it is to a generous and affectionate mind, to be treated so cruelly and unworthily. To deny a common beggar your bounty which he asks, can only be depriving him of a meal; but to give bountifully to a common beggar, and to deny assistance to your friend, is the highest gratification to a proud and cruel disposition.

Let me add, also, that, if it has been in your power to act according to either of the foregoing methods, the more cruelly you have used your friend, the more liberal must you be of your slander and abuse upon him, in order to justify your own proceedings.

To ruin a man by imposing on his generosity and good-nature, and then to laugh at him; to insult your distressed friend with reproaches, and to wear away his very soul by insults, under the mask of kindness; may be called the RACKS, the TORTURES, of friendship. I shall, therefore, quit such deep proceedings, and come to the lighter, finer strokes, more suited to the directions given in all the other connections. As my instructions, also, have been, hitherto, chiefly directed to my female readers, I will pursue the same method; especially as there is, in female friendship, a much more intimate connection, and more frequent opportunities of practising the subtle strokes of teazing, than amongst the men. If, therefore, my fair readers will be so good as to adapt the directions for the choice of a friend, to their own use, I will beg the men, as far as they can, to adapt to their practice the instructions contained in the remaining part of this chapter.

The natural connection on which to found friendship, seems to be that of having sprung from the same parents, having sucked the same milk, having had the same education, and being joined by interest as well as blood. Some friendships of this kind have been very exemplary : but yet it is so very common for brothers and sisters to fight and scratch when they are children, to live a life of quarrelling and snarling when they are grown up; to hate and envy each other with such inveteracy as admits of no disguise ; that it is not to such I address my instructions. However, should two sisters choose to play at friendship, whilst one of them considers the other as her property or dupe, to such these my rules may be of some service.

When you have fixed on a friend, by

the directions already given, endeavour
to engage her affections by all the kind
and obliging methods you can invent.

When you are very certain, that you
are really become the object of her warm-
est friendly affection, and that her chief
joy and pleasure is placed in your company,
and in your satisfaction, try how a change
of temper will agree with her: grow very
melancholy and peevish to every one
around you, except to this friend; but, to
her, still express great love and fondness:
nay, you may frequently suffer yourself
to be talked out of your peevishness and
ill-humour, by her cheerful endeavours to
amuse you. To see this change of temper
in you will grieve her to the heart; but
still, while she finds it is in her power to
relieve your complaints, and to raise your
dejected spirits, she will herself, sometimes, feel such an overflowing of joy, as
will repay her for any trouble, fatigue, or
pain, that she may have undergone. Let

her go on some time in this situation; for she will, by her own compassion, entangle herself too strongly ever to break loose from your chains; although you should hereafter treat her with the most barefaced disregard, insolence, and inhumanity.

Prosperity is, indeed, the proper time to exert insolence; but adversity is the time to engage the affections of the tender and compassionate, so as to make your insolence to them in prosperity more sharply felt.

But it is time now to turn the tables; to be extremely cheerful and good-humoured to all around you; and to be melancholy, peevish, and ill-humoured, only with your friend.

Make your company so unpleasant, that she shall have no enjoyment in it; and then perpetually upbraid her with not choosing to be always with you.

As it has been already advised to upbraid people with their real misfortunes, as being

their own fault; so do you, on the other
hand, if you come to any mishap through
your own folly and obstinacy, not believe
your own ears or eyes, if your friend is
tender and kind to you. What I mean is
this,—If she will not take the part of one
of my scholars, by adding affliction to the
afflicted; do you say to her, that, for all
her frequent visits, and kind words, yet
you know, that, in her heart, she does not
pity you; because she thinks your misfortunes are owing to your own misconduct.
Then begin to rail most vehemently at
the hard heartedness of the world, the
cruelty of ALL friends; and you must ob-
stinately refuse to be comforted with her
utmost endeavours to please and comfort
you.

Tell your friend all sorts of spiteful
stories, that you have heard concerning
her; by which means you may vent your
own spleen, and yet hide the rancour
of your intention, under the pretence of

disbelieving all such calumny; railing, also, at the ill-nature of the wicked, censorious world you live in.

It has ever been held a part of friendship, for friends to tell each other, in a gentle manner, of those faults which it is in their power to rectify. You also, my good pupil, may tell your friend, not only of every fault, but of every human frailty she happens to have: but, be sure, let it not be in an obliging or tender manner. Let it be the effect of some sudden displeasure against her; and you may take that opportunity, also, of telling her as many shocking truths, exaggerated by unkindness, as you can possibly muster up. Should she remonstrate or complain of your unkind words, you must give her this answer, That, truly, you could not, nor would, flatter any one.

For remember, that flattery is only to be used in order to draw somebody in, on whom you may exercise the utmost

brutality, under the name of plain-
dealing.

Never mind whether your friend has
really any faults or not: for you may
falsly accuse her of as many as ever you
please. Be very liberal of your unjust
suspicions, and false accusations; as they
are the daggers which give the deepest
wounds from the hand of a friend. Let
not a twenty years experience of the
truth and fidelity of your friend, prevent
your loading her with the most unjust
suspicions, and accusing her with thoughts
and designs towards you, of which you
either do know, or, at least, ought to
know, that she is perfectly incapable.
This is most nobly grating to a generous
mind: for truly it is said, that *those inju-
ries go nearest to us, that we neither deserve
nor expect.*

It is very possible to hurt your friend
by an extravagant over-strained com-
mendation of some person or other for

some particular good quality which you
have lately been pleased to accuse her
with the want of : but take care that your
accusation was a false one, or else the
whole joke will be lost.

When you have exhausted all your
stock of suspicions, accusations, &c. against
your friend, or have a mind for a little
variety in your practice, there is no better
sport, than to abuse every creature that
you know your friend has any regard for :
but measure out such abuse in its due
proportion; namely, give the greatest
share to that person or persons whom
you know to be most esteemed by your
friend.

When you see your domestics very
ready to observe your commands, it is no
uncommon way, to complain that you can
get nothing done, unless you do it yourself. But as servants generally regard not
such sayings, and often laugh at your
anger and peevishness behind your back,

It would be much better to say this to a friend, whom you see very assiduous to do every thing in her power to serve you.

When a person so thoroughly loves his friend, that it is one of his greatest pleasures to serve, to please, or to amuse him; he cannot, it is true, want thanks for every thing he does; nay, he will be so far from it, that nothing could be more unpleasant to him, than to receive such perpetual acknowledgments for his kindness: yet there is a manner of overlooking such constant endeavours, which is not only mortifying, but very grating, and which I would have you, my good pupil, not fail to practise. But if ever it has been in your power to do the least service to your friend, you may puff and blow; you may magnify the trouble you have taken; and you may praise your own friendly disposition and good-nature, till you have forced from your friend thanks and acknowledgments enough to repay you for having conferred the greatest favour in the world.

Should you also have desired your friend to transact some affair for you, and she, notwithstanding her utmost care and diligence, should fail in her negotiations; do you not fail to blame her for the faults of others; and say, that you know it was all owing to some neglect in her, and her want of inclination to serve you. Add also, that you would trouble her no more: and here properly will come in your lamentation, that you can get nothing done for you, unless you do it yourself.

We have an old English proverb (I wish it more delicately expressed) which says, that *proffered service*, &c. Keep this proverb constantly in your head, and let your friend daily experience the truth of it: for whatever she does to divert, to please, or to serve you, be sure, in the first place, to be neither diverted nor pleased with it; and, in the next place, make out, if possible, that her voluntary endeavours to serve you were of the highest disservice to you. Nay, you may add (if you think she is in a humour to bear it), that you suppose she did this thing, with a design to plague, vex, and distress you.

There is a story in David Simple, of a man who saved another from drowning; but, in dragging him out of the water, happened to hurt the tip of his ear. The man, whose life was saved, had by the next day forgot the service that had been done him, and made most heavy complaints about the pain he felt in his ear. The example of this man may be of great use: for if ever your friends do any thing to serve you, never rest till you have found out some omission in them, by which you have suffered some trifling inconvenience. Of this complain most loudly, without ever mentioning one word of the benefit or emolument you may have received.

Should your friend, through neglect or

inadvertency, have really done something
that was disagreeable, or inconvenient to
you, for which she is heartily vexed; and
therefore, confessing herself in fault, should
ask your pardon for it; you may answer,
that you very readily forgive her; for it
was not your way, to be long angry with
your friends. Besides, you may say, that
you did not think her half so much to
blame, as some *other folks*, by whose example and instigation she used you in this
cruel manner. This reproachful pardon
will certainly draw some answer from
your friend, and you may contrive to
keep on bickering on this irksome subject,
till you have put her into a passion. Then
by your own coolness may you get the
better of her, and irritate her on, till you
have thrown her so much into the wrong,
that she shall again be obliged to ask your
pardon; which you may delay or grant,
just as you find her temper will bear.

Keep as strong a command over your

own passions, I mean those of anger and
resentment, as possible. First, that you
yourself may never be thrown off your
guard; and, next, that you may the better
counterfeit those very passions. For it is
as true of anger as it is of love, that none
can feign it so well, as those who are free
from its power.

Great sport may sometimes be made
out of a passionate person; but it is like
playing with edged tools; they chance
now-and-then to fetch the blood; and you
will frequently, as we say, have the worst
end of the staff; therefore my advice is,
that you choose for your friend a person
of a mild and patient disposition; one not
easily provoked, nor ever giving way to
wrath. You may then safely pretend
often, to throw yourself into violent passions. You may accuse the patient sufferer with cunning and art, in putting on
a calmness (you may say) only to insult
you. Nevertheless, you may boldly insult

her, with some such words as these: "I
" suppose you admire your own wisdom!
" I suppose you think me a passionate
" fool, and provoke me in this manner
" only to expose me!" Thus will you
turn the tables, and make her endeavour
to sooth you. Nay, if she loves a quiet
life, she will, if she finds you will not
be pacified without it, ask your pardon,
instead of your asking hers, for having
indulged your own fractiousness, and for
having abused her for nothing. By this
practice you will also have the world on
your side, from that favourite maxim
(which it is not our interest to contradict),
that passionate people are always the best
natured.

There is one precept extremely essential to this art, but of such general use,
that it is difficult to know under which
head to place it; for it equally serves
every connection. It has been hinted at
in the advice to parents; but, pray, let it

not be omitted amongst friends: this is,
never to give a kind or cheerful reception
to the person who has been some time
absent. If the person is any way your
dependent, sour looks, and severe repri-
mands, are proper: but if it is your husband or friend, upbraidings and reproaches
for absence will be the most teazing method you can pursue.

There is one circumstance, which may
give you a most delightful opportunity of
teazing your friend, and which is generally practised in most families, where
there are a number of young female
friends; I mean where one young lady
has a lover.

If you find, that all the coquetry you
can exert, that all the arts you can use, to
render yourself agreeable, and by that
means to rob your friend of her lover,
should fail, and he should still remain her
admirer, you must comfort yourself for
your disappointment, by the following
ingenious methods:

You must exert the whole power of what is called raillery on your friend, for every the least additional ornament she bestows on her person, whenever she expects her lover. You must noddle, and laugh, and pretend to be very merry, and tell her how extremely becoming such a riband is, and how prettily adapted to her complexion such a coloured gown is; and you may say, " It is easy to guess, my " dear, by your smirking countenance, " who is expected to-day." As few girls have courage enough to own the truth, namely, that they really wish to appear as agreeable as they can in the eyes of their lover, your friend will be greatly teazed and vexed by this your raillery. Nay, if she happens to have any great degree of bashfulness, she will even omit many points of dress, to avoid your jokes; you may also attack her with all your smartness, on any little effort she makes in conversation, to appear sprightly and

agreeable; by which means she will be so
much afraid of your raillery, that she will
appear to the greatest disadvantage, where
she would most wish to please. When you
have thus got her down, you may yourself
dress out, and talk away, and have one
more trial of skill, perhaps, for becoming
her rival.

If you know of any little failings she
has, which she would wish to conceal (at
least, till she had rendered herself, by many
real good qualities, so much esteemed by
her lover, that if he was a good-natured
man, he would forgive them), be sure to
bring them all out before him as soon as
possible, in hopes of preventing any violent attachment. This has been sometimes practised with success, even among
the men; for I once knew a match entirely broke off (and the man was almost
distracted for the loss of his mistress) only
by his friend's saying to him, before the
lady, " I wish you was hanged, Jack; for

" you kept me awake all last night by
" your confounded snoring."

If your friend should not be quite sure
of her lover, but he should be one of those
men, who without any positive declaration
of love had engaged her by many acts of
gallantry, to live in daily hopes of such a
declaration; then have you a fine scope
for working and teazing her to death,
seconding in a manner all his tricks, either
by raising those hopes, or alarming her
fear. And you will have the rod of mortification so strongly in your hands on
that subject, that you will seldom need
any other exercise of your power.

Ill health, a weak frame of body, and
low spirits, are the unhappy lot of many
people; from whence they reasonably
claim both favour and indulgence from
the good-natured part of mankind: this
tempts numbers to affect those ills, in
order to claim the same indulgence. The
proper use to be made of distinguishing

the real sick from the counterfeit, you will find in my general instructions, &c.

If you are blessed with a larger share of health and spirits than your neighbours, be properly insolent thereon (for people may be health-proud, as well as purse-proud); and you may frequently declare, that you do not believe, that ill-health comes to any one, but through their own self-indulgence. This will do very well amongst all your acquaintance; but will be better towards your friend, if she should be of a weakly constitution; but if she is not, then you had better take the part yourself of affected weakness; as many emoluments may arise therefrom.

There are two ways of plaguing your friends by your requests to them, very different in themselves; but both of excellent use; and are as follow:

If your friend be of such an obliging, complying temper, as to be unwilling to deny you any thing you ask; and perfectly averse, also, to contradicting any proposal, that would give you pleasure; you may, in the first place, make all sorts of preposterous requests to her; nor value how many absurd and improper things you make her do, in compliance with your whims. In the next place, you must study her temper, to find out what is agreeable or disagreeable to her: then persecute her daily, with proposals to do something or other, that is highly unpleasant to her; by which means she must either live an uncomfortable life, from never doing any thing she likes; or she must be eternally contradicting your proposals, and refusing your requests; which may, perhaps, be more irksome to her, than any disagreeable thing you can desire her to do.

The other method of requests is this: .

If your friend be so assiduous to serve and please you, that, by making your concerns her own, she, as much as possible,

prevents even your very wishes, you may
often make such ungracious and disobliging requests, as will be truly grating to a
friendly disposition. This is a very refined stroke, and great part of its force
lies in the manner of wording your requests, and the tone of your voice in
expressing such your desires. There is an
honest earnestness, with which people
may, sometimes, remind their friends,
either of their intentions, or promises, to
serve them; and there is a manner of
requesting, which carries with it neither
insult nor suspicion. But, drawing up
your head very high, you must begin your
requests thus:—" Let me beseech you—
" Let me entreat you—Pray do me the
" favour—I beg you would not forget me
" so much, as to neglect doing so or so,
" &c." To which, if your friend (a little
hurt) should tell you, that it was some-
what unkind in you to ask her, *in such a
manner*, to do what you was convinced

M

she intended to do without any asking at
all; then may you lie snug, and, some
time after, play her a most noble back-
stroke; for when next you want her to
serve you in something which it is impossible for her to guess at without being
told, you must omit asking her to do it,
or giving her the least hint of the matter:
now make up some heavy inconvenience
that you have sustained; complain of
your great hardship, in not having the
advantage of the common assistance of
friendship where it is most wanted, from
that strange oddness in your friend's temper, that she would *never* be asked to do
any thing, without growing angry, and
putting herself into a violent passion about
it. You may say, also, that, for your part,
all you wished was, that your friend would
tell you how you could oblige her; and
you would fly to the Indies to do her any
service. Then add as many more warm
professions of friendship (as they are

called) as you please. This, in all probability, will have a good chance for turning
the tables, for making her ask *your* pardon; and she will, most likely, comply
with any terms you shall make, rather
than see you uneasy.

If this friend, or property of yours,
should happen to have any other connections, you must endeavour to embarrass
her as much as possible: for, if she tells
you, that she is to do such a thing to serve
one person, such a thing to oblige another, be sure to make some direct opposite request; so that she shall be certain
of disobliging either you, or somebody
else.

If it should be in your power to do this
friend of your's any service, and she should
ever make any requests to you, be very
sparing of absolutely denying such requests, for fear of giving her an open
cause of complaint against you: but grant
all such favours in such a disobliging and

ungracious manner, as shall destroy all the pleasure of your friend.

This method of granting favours in a disgustful manner, is one of our chief springs, and must be practised in as many connections as you possibly can introduce it.

But in this, generally, granting your friend's requests, mistake me not so far, as to do her any very essential service; especially such a one as might raise her, in rank or fortune, above yourself; for to see one's dearest friend get the start of one in any thing, is too much for such friendship to bear. Therefore, rather lose your friend by a refusal, than undergo the above-mentioned horrid mortification.

You need not be at the trouble of racking your invention for spiteful things to say, in order to vex all your acquaintance and friends; for if you will only be sure never to suppress any one thing that comes uppermost, I will engage (if you are a true scholar of mine) the business will be very completely done.

The affecting low spirits and dejection, in order to afflict your friend, has been already advised; but the affectation of very high spirits is no unpleasant conceit, when you have worked your friends to oil; or, as Shakspeare says, *Fool'd them to the top of their bent.*

Although you are to vex, plague, and abuse your friends, as much as ever the power you have over them, by their affections, will bear; yet be sure to seem very jealous of any other person's using them ill: this makes the appearance of great zeal for their service; and (blinded by their love for you) they will almost persuade themselves, that it is impossible for you to use them cruelly, when you are so alarmed for fear of their suffering any ill treatment from another.

In like manner, when you have been harassing a servant all day off his legs, you may pity the poor fellow so extremely, and be so very sparing of his labour, that you will not suffer him to go three steps on a necessary errand for your *friend,* for fear of over-fatiguing him.

Should your friend seldom dispute any thing with you, never find any fault with you, nor ever remonstrate against your unkind, your disobliging, and your disagreeable ways, set this down to the account of your own goodness and perfection, and not to the patient forbearance of your friend. Yet you may boldly act in consequence of knowing the latter to be the truth of the case, by continuing and persisting in such a teazing and tormenting behaviour, as little less than the patience of Job could bear with or endure.

In short, my good pupils, if you study well my instructions; and, from these my outlines, finish for yourselves a complete system for the practice of tormenting your friends; I will be bold to pronounce of you, what Claudian has already so well expressed to my hands.

Talem progenies hominum si prisca tulisset,
Pirithoum fugeret Theseus: offensus Orestem
Desereret Pylades, odissèt Castora Pollux.

                                    In Rvf. lib. i. v. 107.

CHAPTER IV.

*To your Good Sort of People; being an
Appendage to the foregoing Chapter.*

Says Dean Swift, in his poem of Cadenus
and Vanessa,

> 'Tis an old maxim in the schools,
> That vanity's the food of fools:
> Yet, now-and-then, your men of wit
> Will condescend to take a bit.

And may we not, with some propriety,
apply this to our ingenious art of tormenting?

It is acknowledged, that the chief adepts
in our science are those only who are
blessed with a proper share of spite and
malignity: yet, observation has taught me,
that many a good man, and many a good
woman, who have possessed numberless
virtues, have, now-and-then, recreated

their spirits with a small touch of this pleasant sport: and although they have not absolutely inflicted a strong torment, yet have gone so far in the art of teazing, as greatly to perplex and disconcert the best laid intentions for giving them pleasure.

An obliging, complying temper, as shewn in the last chapter, may be finely worked and teazed, by being forced either to do what is disagreeable, or to be always saying *no*: but the same temper and disposition, by never saying *no*, may very much distress others, as well as itself. To explain my meaning, take two or three short stories; and then, gentle reader, you will be the best judge of the justice of this observation.

What gave me the hint for these kind of reflections, was the account which a young lady (whom I will call Felicia) was giving me of her friend Hermia; who, she said, was the best woman in the world;

but, from too great a compliance in her temper, was perpetually falling into inconveniences herself, and making all her friends around her miserable.

" Hermia (said Felicia) is a woman " whom I love and esteem as my own " soul. Her real charity, her benevolence, " her gentleness of disposition, shew me, " that there is at least one human being, " in whom every human virtue is centred. " So thoroughly am I blessed by the " warmth of her friendship, and the kind- " ness of her heart, that I should pro- " nounce myself a monster of ingratitude, " if I could move or act with any view " but for her pleasure. Her greatest de- " light is pleasing and obliging all her " friends; but, from an unwillingness to " give trouble, she never requests any " person to do any one thing in the world " for her; fearing, I believe, that she " should rob her friends of some pleasure " of their own. Yet, as it is impossible to

" know her whole mind so well as she
" knows it herself, there must, sometimes,
" be such omissions to her, as will put her
" to inconvenience, and grieve her friends
" to behold. In the beginning of our ac-
" quaintance, this passive disposition of
" my friend Hermia often gave me great
" pain: for as she is so very averse to
" contradicting any proposal, that she
" will do a thing the most contrary to her
" own inclinations, rather than thwart
" another's, I have frequently found my-
" self the cause of giving her great pain
" and uneasiness, when it has been the
" farthest from my inclinations so to do.
" Hermia is far from being of a weakly
" constitution, but has very strange disor-
" ders in her head, for which she is ad-
" vised to walk long walks; and this,
" from her good health in all other re-
" spects, she is very well able to perform.
" We were one day, in the country, to
" walk (in very hot weather) home to her

" own house, and the distance was about
" four miles. We were setting out while
" the sun was yet very high; on which I
" proposed to her (fearing, indeed, that
" the scorching heat would hurt her head)
" to stay till the cool of the evening. I
" observed to her, also, how beautiful the
" moon, being that night at the full,
" would look through the high trees, and
" in the clear river by whose banks we
" were to pass. Hermia made not the
" least objection, but readily consented;
" and we had, to me, a most agreeable
" and pleasant walk; nor did she seem
" less delighted with the various beauties
" of this rural scene, than myself. But,
" as soon as she came into the house, she
" was very much disordered, and really
" ready to faint away: seeing me exces-
" sively concerned, she told me her com-
" plaint would soon go off; for it was
" only the common effect of walking in
" the moon-light. It was for that reason

" (added she), that I was desirous of walk-
" ing in the middle of the day; and, in-
" deed, should have done so, if you, Felicia,
" had not proposed staying till the cool
" of the evening. I gently complained
" of her compliance with any proposal of
" mine, in a case where her own health
" was concerned; and she candidly ac-
" knowledged herself to blame: she pro-
" mised, also, to speak her mind more
" freely another time. But, before our
" discourse was ended, she called for some
" water to drink; and a bottle of wine
" standing by, I desired her to pour a
" little into the water, as I feared she was
" too warm with her walk, to venture on
" so cool a liquor as water just come from
" the pump. She readily took my advice,
" filled the glass half full of water, drank
" it off, and in less than five minutes fell
" into a strong convulsion-fit. I was half
" at my wits-end. I sent for her physician,
" and he, on seeing Hermia, asked, if she

" had not tasted some wine, which, he
" said, always threw her into these kinds
" of fits. With pain and anguish I re-
" plied, that she had drank a large glass
" of wine and water, and that I had given
" it her. It was some hours before she
" could be brought to her senses. From
" that day, I attempted not any more to
" complain; for I found how much in
" vain it was for me to remonstrate
" against this her cruel proceeding to-
" wards herself; nor was there any way
" left for me, but, by a constant observ-
" ance and watchfulness to prevent her
" hurting her own health, in order to
" oblige others."

The good-natured Felicia told several
more instances of the same kind, expressing the most anxious concern for her
friend Hermia's sufferings, on account of
that over-compliance and obligingness of
disposition, of which she was possessed.
But let me whisper it into my friend

Hermia's ear, that, I think, in her, I spy some marks of a love to our sport. If it was possible, that the moonlight walk was taken, and the wine was drank, on purpose to give anxiety to Felicia, I could do no other than pronounce Hermia to be one of my very best pupils—To be got even amongst that upper class of those, who are capable of hanging themselves to spite their neighbours. But as I have reason to believe, that she really deserves the other part of the character given her by Felicia, and that she indulges her own compliance of disposition, to the distress of herself, and all around her, through a thoughtlessness of the consequence of her own actions, I readily dismiss her from my upper class: but I still insist upon it, that she ignorantly fights under my banner, and is one of the flying squadron, for whose honour and service this chapter is intended.

Hermia, by the male part of my readers,

perhaps, may be presumed (as she is a woman) to be weak, and not capable of considering the force of her own words, or the consequences of her own actions: but what shall we say to Albertus?

Albertus is a man of great sense, an uncommon genius, and so very mild and gentle in his disposition, that happy are all those who are nearly connected with him. To enumerate all his real good qualities, would (with as much truth as ever it was said) swell this volume to a folio. He has a friend, Horatio, who has the highest veneration, and the justest regard for him; whose chief delight is in his company; and whose greatest pleasure would be that of being able, by any means, to add to the ease and satisfaction of his friend. But Horatio, like poor Felicia, is perpetually mortified by finding himself in some way or other the cause, the unhappy undesigning cause, of Albertus's distress.

One day, seeing Albertus ill, and hearing him say, that he must be in the city the next morning on very important business, Horatio asked him, if he could not commission him to transact this business for him. Albertus thanked him; but said, he feared it might prevent some business or pleasure of his own. Horatio assured him he had no business of his own that day, nor any pleasure, but an invitation to a morning concert, which was an engagement too trifling for him to put in competition with being of any service to his most distant acquaintance, and much more so with his best friend: he begged, therefore, that Albertus would inform him of the business.

Albertus hesitated some time; then said, that he had recollected some circumstances, which made it impossible for any one but himself to transact the affair; and he must therefore either go himself,

N

or put it off till another day, when he was in better health.

Horatio knowing the sincerity of his own intentions to serve his friend, and not doubting that Albertus, from long experience, knew it as well as himself (having also no desire of making a shew of overstrained importunity, where he thought his offer could not be accepted), took his leave, wishing him health to transact his business, and success in the execution of it. Albertus, with great seeming good-humour, returned his good wishes, by hoping he would have much pleasure in his musical entertainments.

The next day, Horatio goes to the concert in the morning, and visits his friend in the afternoon. He finds him a little mended in his health; but appearing under great vexation of mind. He hastily and anxiously enquires the cause of his distress. Albertus answers, that he had

not been in health or spirits, that morning, to go into the city; that he had sent
a man to transact the business for him,
and by the blunder of that man he had
lost two hundred pounds.

" Since you found it was possible for
" another to transact your business for
" you, why, my good friend (cries Ho-
" ratio), would you not send to me?"

Albertus mildly answers, " You was
" engaged, Sir, at a concert—you are
" very fond of music—I cannot bear, for
" my own convenience, to debar my
" friends of their *pleasures*."

Oh, Albertus, Albertus, honestly answer
me this question. If you believed your
friend's regard for you sincere, was you
not robbing him of his greatest pleasure,
by refusing him an opportunity of doing
you an essential service?

It must be confessed, that it is not con-
sistent with the characters to whom this
chapter is addressed, to say grating or ill-

natured things, with a design to torment;
nor can they, by any means, be supposed
to feign sickness, or low spirits, for the
above-mentioned purpose. But (counte-
nanced by custom) they may, if they
please, when they are really sick or low-
spirited, indulge the highest degree of
fretfulness, peevishness, and ill-humour;
and may also, from a thorough carelessness of their words and expressions, give
some very good random shots, without
positively taking aim.

A habit of saying fretful things, without strictly examining into the truth of
them, will bring a person into a belief of
their reality. As for instance: If you
frequently say, that nobody cares for you,
it will not be long, before you will imagine all mankind your enemies: or if any
person should once or twice make you
wait, should miss an appointment, or the
like, by telling them that they *always* do
so, you may work yourself into such a

belief of its truth, that a repeated behaviour to the contrary can with difficulty bring you to acknowledge, and be convinced of your mistake.

Whilst your good sort of people take the allowance that is given to the sick, of indulging every captious and peevish humour that will rise, or attempt to arise, in almost every mind; it is not from such, that I fear the overthrow of our art. But the person uniformly cautious, both in words and actions, never to give the least offence, is our greatest and most powerful enemy. And that we have some such enemies abroad, experience has taught me to confess. Nay, what a strange creature did I once hear of! A young lady of title and fortune, who had servants, friends, and dependents, at her command, was afflicted with a painful disorder (which at last deprived her of life) for near twelve years; yet never took the opportunity of one of those advantages, to say a cross or

fretful thing to any one! Though born to
a high station, she chose a private life;
the influence of her example, therefore,
was not to be greatly dreaded. But what
shall we say, if such a behaviour should
even now shine forth, not far from a
throne? If there should now be a living
example of a person, that, with as much
exterior power as any one can possess,
next to our Sovereign himself, and with
as much interior power as the affections
of a whole nation can give, never exerts
that power, but for the pleasure and benefit, instead of the torment, of all her dependents? Should we not, my dear pupils,
alarmed by the danger of such a shining
exemplar, all assemble together, in order,
by some envious detraction, to pull down
this our greatest enemy? Alas! she is
above our reach! Therefore have we no
hope left, but in trying to reverse an old
general observation, and in arduously
endeavouring to shew, that these our

precepts will be more forcible towards promoting the love of tormenting, than the most royal and illustrious example will be, towards inculcating and teaching every Christian virtue.

ESSAY

ON THE

ART OF TORMENTING.

GENERAL RULES, &c.

GENERAL RULES

For plaguing all your Acquaintance; with the Description of a Party of Pleasure.

T H E part my pupils are to act in plague-
ing all their acquaintanc, could not, with
any propriety, be placed under either of
the foregoing divisions: for their power,
in this case, arises more from custom and
good-breeding, than from exterior authority, or affectionate hold of the heart.

Yet, in one sense, it may be said to
have a place in each of the foregoing divisions: for there is no better method of
plaguing your acquaintance, than so to
time the exercise of both your exterior
and interior power, as to be insufferably
troublesome to all around you.

But, let their methodical place be where
they will, my directions are as follow:

As you cannot bind your common acquaintance to you by any of the methods already mentioned, it will be necessary for you to put on such a deportment, as will render you, sometimes, very agreeable, in order to prevent your being entirely deserted; except you should happen to be the indulged wife of an uxorious husband, and then you may exert the most bare-faced ill-humour and insolence, that you are capable of; for he must and will support you in all your tricks and impertinence, let them be ever so preposterous and absurd.

By all means avoid an evenness of behaviour. Be, sometimes, extremely glad to see people; and, at other times, let your behaviour be hardly within the rules of good-breeding.

If you are acquainted with persons of punctilio, don't directly affront them; but contrive continually to nettle them, and keep them on the fret, by such a carelessness and neglect, as will take away all their pleasure in conversation : whereas, on the other hand, for that part of your acquaintance who are easy-tempered people, who love civil freedom, and stand not on forms and ceremonies, persecute them with officious complaisance : nor ever let them rest five minutes in the same place; but press them continually to change it for one that you hope is more commodious.

Never let the time of dinner pass in quiet. For if there be not a surly husband to find fault with his wife, and put all the company in pain for her, then let the wife herself find fault with the dressing of every dish; send *this* down to be more done; send *that* from the table, for being rotten roasted; and keep the whole company in such a confusion, as shall at least take away their pleasure, if not their appetites to their dinner.

Suffer your servants to be as negligent,

and as rude to your visitors, as they please; nor ever observe whether they give them, at table, clean or dirty glasses, knives, plates, &c. They will undoubtedly be the better to you for this your indulgence in suffering them to plague and insult your friends.

If you lend your coach, wink at your coachman's insolence or impertinence: for it will save your wheels from being worn out in the service of any one besides yourself.

There is no better use of having your children noisy and troublesome, than this of plaguing all your acquaintance: for you may suffer them, when you have visitors, to make such a racket, that you cannot hear one another speak; let them, also, with their greasy fingers, soil and besmear your visitors cloaths; cut their hoods, capuchins, or tippets (if laid in the window), with scissars; put their fingers, and dirty noses (if you are drinking tea), into the cream-pot, and drivel over the sugar; throw the remainder of the cream over somebody's clean gown; climb up upon the chair, and thrust some bread and butter* down the ladies backs; and, in short, be more troublesome and offensive, than either squirrels, parrots, or monkies.

You have two ways of acting, on this agreeable behaviour of your children: one is, to put on an absolute blindness, and to take not the least notice of any one enormity they commit: the other is to find perpetual faults with them before company (if you know they are head-strong enough not to mind you); and, by correcting them for every step they take,

---

* To avoid the absurdity that must appear in this passage, when the wheel of fashion shall have brought the ladies to dress themselves in the decent manner of their great-grandams; and, by that means, shall have rendered this trick of the child's impracticable; be it noted, that, in the year 1752, it was a general fashion for ladies to appear naked *behind*, almost half-way down their backs.

you will yourself become as troublesome to your visitors, as the children themselves, without your correction, possibly could be.

If you see people particularly cheerful, rack your invention to the utmost, to find some method of damping their mirth and good-humour: for, should you happen to have no friend, husband, &c. in company, on whom to exercise your power; yet, to destroy the mirth of a common acquaintance is some joy, although not the greatest, to a truly malevolent heart.

There are several good tricks of mortification, which you may apply properly, by attending to people's characters and dispositions, so as to find out what they most value and pride themselves upon. Agreeableness, at least, if not beauty of person, is strongly the wish of every one, even men as well as women; and, from that wish, people are so desirous of believing themselves possessed of it, that

personal strokes of mortification seldom
miss their aim; although less outward
resentment is shewn in that, than in any
other case.

If Tom Neverout, who doats on being
thought a wit, should look pleased with
the approbation of the company for having said a good thing, you may say, that,
a month ago, you heard Jack Jolterhead
(whom Tom despises to his soul) say the
same thing: on this, the laugh of approbation will be turned into a laugh of contempt, poor Tom will be mortified, and
you will be applauded for your wit. Tom
will be more inwardly vexed, than he will
outwardly express, for fear of being again
laughed at; and you will have him, all
that evening, at your mercy; for you may
revive the laugh against him at any time,
only by patting him on the shoulder, and
saying, " Come, honest Tom, have you
" no other good thing of Jack Jolterhead's
" to pass off for your own, and to divert

o

" the company ?" This, I have been told,
is what they call being smart in company;
and, if I might be forgiven the heinous sin
of a pun, I should suppose that expression
arose from the smarting pain you give to
another by this mortifying sort of wit.

To women, your best way is to attack
them about their cloaths. When you see
them pleased with any gown, cap, or
riband, that they have on, you may drop
it out (as if by chance), " that it was
" exactly such a gown, as you saw Mrs.
" Meagre in at Sadler's Wells;" carefully
remembering, on these occasions, to name
either some very frightful, unfashionable,
or ridiculous character.

Be continually begging all your acquaintance to help you to servants; to
recommend you to mantua-makers, mil-
liners, with shops of all kinds. The old,
experienced ones, who can guess at your
intentions by such requests, will decline
giving you any such recommendations;

but your unexperienced, good-natured
people, will readily undertake to send you
a servant, or to recommend some person
in business, hoping, thereby, to please
you, and serve and encourage some indus-
trious tradesman. Fail not to employ the
person thus recommended: if it is a servant, let him soon be discharged, with
great disgrace; nor ever let your friend
escape being upbraided with recommending one of the worst of servants. Complain of the mantua-maker, that she
spoiled you a suit of cloaths, and stole
several yards of your silk. If a milliner
is recommended to you, you may rally
your friend in the following manner:
" Surely, my dear, you sent Mrs. ——
" the milliner to me out of a joke; for
" you could not imagine, that I would
" appear such a *fright*, as that aukward
" creature, of your recommendation,
" would have made me!" As to shops, of
all kinds, you need not buy any thing at

any place to which you are recommended; but you may complain to your friends, that, by their recommendation, you was like to have been cheated most intolerably, had it not been for your own great judgment, by which you plainly perceived that the person asked double the worth of the goods; and that you could buy them for half the price at any other shop in town.

As the time in which you can exercise your power over a common acquaintance, is no more than a visit will allow; and as that visit, should you grow too troublesome to be endured, can be shortened; your best method would be to propose frequent parties of pleasure; for in such expeditions lies the largest scope for being troublesome; and the company, by this expedient, are in a manner bound together, at least one day: to this sort of sport, therefore, shall the remainder of this chapter be directed.

In most parties of pleasure, you have commonly one or two, who, by feigned fits, head-achs, frights, &c. destroy all the comfort of the day: but, should there be one amongst you, who, from a real weak constitution, is not able to undertake what the healthy part of the company may propose, then postpone those common tricks above to a better opportunity; and fly all at once upon your present game.

Make all sorts of proposals unfit for an unhealthy person to undertake; as walking in the heat of the day, staying out in the damps of the evening, hurrying from one place to another without any respite; or propose any other frolic, to which your invention may help you: if your proposals are complied with, you half kill your victim; but if she should object to these things, you may accuse her of affectation, and a design of spoiling company: or, instead of outward reproaches, you may shew, by a sneer, that you do not believe

she is ill. You may also say, that you are
less able to walk, ride, bear heat, cold, &c.
than she is; but, for your part, you do not
love giving trouble, nor ever make the
least complaint, although you are half-
dead. But, in this rule, be sure not to
mistake your person, and, instead of tormenting a poor sick wretch, detect a true
sister of the art: yet such a mistake is
not much to be apprehended, as there are
as certain marks by which to distinguish
a sister of our science, as a brother of the
Masonry: but far be it from me to di-
vulge these arcana; I too much revere this
our noble art, to expose its inmost myste-
ries to vulgar eyes. And here give me
leave, since I have mentioned Freema-
sonry, to observe, that the practitioners
of our art are, I believe, more numerous
than the Masons, and the art itself of still
greater antiquity than theirs. They boast
their institution but from the tower of
Babel, whereas I doubt not but I could

bring proof, that our's is derived from our grand and general mother EVE herself.

In all parties of pleasure, the first thing to be considered is, of how much weight and consequence you are to the rest of the company. If you have in the party no husband, lover, or friend, that will indulge or humour you, it is your best way to enjoy yourself as well as you can; only watching for some favourable opportunity, when there is any dispute, so as to put in your opinion on the weakest side; not out of compassion for the weak, but in order by that means to support and increase the wrangle, and to prevent it, for some minutes at least, from coming to an end. But if (as before observed) you have nobody there that will be hurt by your ill-humour, do not carry it too far, for fear of being mortified by the contempt of the company; as it would be much better, also, to save it for a more convenient opportunity.

If you know yourself to be of some consequence, although not the very principal person of the party, you may, by opposition, make a good deal of sport. You cannot, indeed, carry things so high, as if you was at the helm; but you may dispute every inch of ground with the queen of the day, provided her forces are not strong enough to render her power absolute. If your party is walking, you must love walking fast, if she likes walking leisurely: in a coach, you must love the glasses down, and complain of being suffocated, if she chooses them up: in a boat, be the weather ever so fine, you must beg and entreat to have a tilt, if she likes to be without one: at Vauxhall or Ranelagh, you must be continually teazing the company to go home, if you see them pleased with staying; or you may wait till the proposal is made for going, and, all at once, grow into very high spirits, and complain that they should think of breaking up the party, just as you began to enjoy yourself. In short, keep up in your mind the true spirit of contradiction to every thing that is proposed or done; and although, from want of power, you may not be able to exercise tyranny, yet, by the help of perpetual mutiny, you may heartily torment and vex all there that love you; and be as troublesome as an impertinent fly, to those who care not three farthings about you.

If you are the principal person in the party, that is, if you are young and hand-some, and have a lover with you; or it you are the adored wife of a man who makes an agreeable party on purpose to please you, consisting of his own sisters, and some other ladies and gentlemen who will acknowledge you as their queen; then will your reign for that time be absolute; excepting only the quelling, perhaps, a few rebellions which may hap-pen, if you should chance to have any of the above-mentioned mutineers in company.

The power of a beautiful woman over her lover, may, perhaps, be greater than that of an indulged wife over her husband; but her power over the rest of the company, for many reasons I could give, cannot be half so great. Take, therefore, the instance of the indulged wife. To such I now address myself; and, to make my instructions clearly understood, let us imagine the party made: let us suppose it to consist of yourself, your fond husband, his two sisters, two young gentlemen, and another young lady. A coach and chaise (if you have them not of your own) are hired; you, with your husband and his two sisters, go in the coach; the young lady in the chaise, with one of the gentlemen; who we will suppose to be an admirer of her's; and the other gentleman may ride on his own horse. It would be no bad trick, as soon as you are stepping

into the coach, to say you are suddenly
taken very ill; and so, for that day, dis-
appoint the whole company. But, however, the same party is once more formed;
the day is arrived, and you all sally forth,
in the same order as before, but not with
the same glee; for, after a balk of this
sort, there will always be such a damp on
these kind of expeditions, as takes off half
their joy. We will suppose your plan to
be as follows: you intend to be out three
days; to go directly to Windsor, and
spend the whole day there; to go the
next day to Esher, in order to see those
two beautiful seats, the Duke of New-
castle's, and Mr. Pelham's; to go that night
to Hampton-court; there to discharge
your coach, &c.; and the next day, after
having seen the palace and gardens, to
go down the river in a six-oared barge,
ordered to meet you there, for that purpose. By this means you enjoy all the
beauties of the Thames, with the many

fine seats on its banks; and you propose to close your expedition by calling in the evening both at Ranelagh and Vauxhall.

The weather is fine, and away you go.

When you have travelled about three or four miles, you may begin to be very uneasy, either with being too hot, or too cold, or just what you please: or you may complain, you are so sick with riding in the coach, that you can go no farther. Should the motion of a coach never before have made you sick, yet you may assert it does so now; for married women have always a pretence for complaining of unaccountable disorders. The whole cavalcade, at your command, will stop; and, for the benefit of more air, you immediately displace the young lady in the chaise, especially if you see her pleased with her situation. This may not be very agreeable to the young gentleman; but, out of complaisance to you, the queen of the party, he will not dispute the exchange. This must not hold long, especially, if, passing by, you should hear your husband laughing, or talking in a cheerful manner, in the coach; you must drag him out from thence, but by no means take him into the chaise to you; for then you would leave all the young unmarried folks to themselves: you may plead fear of his driving, and, therefore, beg the young gentleman on horseback to get into the coach, and suffer your husband to ride his horse, that you may have the pleasure of dear Billy's company by the side of the chaise. To this (as it is asked under the mask of fondness) your husband cannot but consent, although he is unfitted by his dress for riding, and perhaps it may also be to him a disagreeable way of travelling. However, as pouts would be the consequence of a refusal, out of the coach he gets, mounts the horse, and rides in the dust to Windsor.

While dinner is getting ready, you walk over the castle; and here you have little to do, but to put on an absolute indifference to every thing that either your husband, or any of the rest of the company, shew you, as being worth your observation. It would be no bad thing, to carry a knotting-bag with you, and to employ your fingers and attention on that as much as possible, whilst the others are employed in admiring the paintings, and other beauties, of that superb castle. But if either of your husband's sisters should desire you to observe any particular picture, as praising the drawing of it, or taking notice how well it expressed such a piece of history; you may say, " That, " indeed, you don't pretend to understand " painting and history, and such *learned* " things; you leave those studies to such " *wise* ladies as they are, who, you sup- " pose, despise her for a weak silly wo- " man." Although you may just give

your sisters one snap, where it lies so
fairly in your way; yet, for the most part,
by no means seem low-spirited, or out of
humour (that does not come in turn yet);
but rather hum a tune, and every now-
and-then seem vastly delighted with some
trifling thing or other, that you meet with,
which ought to be below the notice of a
girl of eight years old.

At dinner you have nothing to do, but
to be as troublesome as you can; to dislike
every thing that is provided, and to send
an hundred ways to get something you
can eat. If there should be any dish your
husband's sisters particularly like, you may
hate the smell of it so much, that it must
be immediately sent from the table.
Should any one take notice, that you
never before disliked that dish; you must
boldly declare, that you always hated and
abhorred it, and had been ready to faint
away twenty times, by its being brought
to the table; but nobody had regard

enough for you, ever to observe what was agreeable or disagreeable to you in any thing. The more false this assertion is, the more likely will you be of carrying your point, that is, of dumb-founding all the company : for should you have eaten very heartily of that very dish, but the very day before, it will only strike the company silent with astonishment at your *very* great assurance.

If your husband be a man of taste and relish for fine prospects, and should have expressed great pleasure, whilst at dinner, with the thought of an evening walk in Windsor park, and on the terrace; if he should also say to you, " My dear, I will " shew you such a view, such a walk, " &c." then lie snug with the thought of playing him a most charming trick, all under the mask of the highest good-humour and fondness. For when you are all setting out for your walk on the terrace, and to the park, you may say to your

husband, as you lean upon his arm, " Bid
" them walk on, my dear, and say you
" and I will follow them." Your fond
husband, without asking your reasons,
will undoubtedly do as you desire, and
away they all go. Then do you run back
into the room where you dined, call to
your husband, and say, " Come hither,
" my dear Billy; let you and I stay here
" and enjoy ourselves, whilst they are
" trudging about, and fatiguing them-
" selves in a great wide park." Should
your husband gently remonstrate, and
hint also, how much pleasanter it would
be to walk out, and how much pleasure
he had proposed in shewing you the prospects, &c. you may fondly hang about
his neck, and declare that no fine prospect,
nor any other amusement, was any pleasure to you, in comparison with his dear
company: that you preferred that paltry
room at an inn, thus sitting alone with
him, before the sight of all the palaces in

P

Europe; and it would be very unkind in him, if he would not indulge you in your request of staying there till the company came in from walking. You need not fear carrying your point by fondling endearments, and trifling good-humour. When the company returns from walking, you must seem in the highest spirits imaginable; and, continuing so all the evening, you may talk in such a manner of the pleasure you enjoyed in their absence, as will put your husband in a sweat for you, and will give the young fellows an opportunity of putting all the young ladies to the blush.

This first day of your expedition your husband has been your chief victim; and that, too, by very little peevishness, but chiefly by exerting a silly childish good-humour.

Now change your method; be very much out of spirits, and take all occasions of bickering and disputing with your husband's sisters.

When you arrive at Esher, and you are all going directly to Claremont, you may declare, that you are not in spirits to walk about the gardens, and you desire to be left sitting in the house. If your husband offers to sit with you, tell him, that you will not on any account confine him; but you think it would be only common good-manners to you, and good-nature to their brother, for his sisters to offer to stay with you; for it was not very fit you should be left by yourself. On this, it is most likely, that one of them will offer to keep you company. Take not any notice, nor seem the least pleased with her civility; but say to your husband, that you are so low-spirited you can enjoy nobody's company; and that the only thing that could amuse you, would be a game at ombre: if therefore he could so far prevail with his sisters, as to persuade them, once in their lives, to give up their own pleasure for your amusement, you should be glad they would make up your party; but you positively insisted upon it, that you would confine no other part of the company: you may add, with a sigh, that you hoped, indeed, you might take that small liberty with your husband's sisters. Then boldly take the cards and counters out of your knotting-bag; for nobody will dare to tell you, that you put them there for that purpose. The rest of the company will have little pleasure in their walk, from this division that you have made; and you must exert as much spleen and ill-humour at cards, as possible, without seeming in the least pleased or obliged by your sisters compliance to your wayward fancies. You may perpetually tell them, that you suppose they wish you hanged, for keeping them from the young fellows; with as many other spiteful things as you can invent. You know that, for fear of offending their brother, they will not contradict you; and you may therefore work

them within an inch of their lives. If you
still continue your low spirits, and pretended fondness for cards, your husband,
and the rest of the company, will give up
all thoughts of seeing Mr. Pelham's ele-
gant gardens; for there can be no enjoyment with such a division of company;
and you will in all probability go directly
to Hampton-court. For fear your husband, and the rest of the company, from
the damp you have thrown upon their
pleasures, should propose returning directly home to London, grow into tolerable spirits, as soon as you come to Hampton-court, and say, that you propose great
pleasure the next day, in going down the
river: you may likewise declare, that
Hampton-court palace was the only place
you wanted to see, on account of the
beauties there, painted by Sir Godfrey
Kneller. After you have, by this declaration, prevented the party from being
broke up, and your coach, chaise, &c.

are all dispatched for London, grow as
wayward, fretful, and peevish, as you possibly can; making it the business of the
company to endeavour at diverting and
amusing you. But be sure to lose this
whole day, by coming into no proposal
for pleasure; that is, putting it off, by
saying, you hope to be in better spirits
to-morrow. Take all opportunities of
shewing your power over your husband's
sisters; and it would be no bad frolic (by
way of making a bustle, and giving them
all the plague and trouble you can), if,
about an hour after you are a-bed, you
was to declare, that you could not sleep in
that bed, and so make your husband get
up, and prevail with his sisters to change
beds with you.

The last day of your expedition is arrived ; you walk over Hampton-court
palace, either with some pleasure, or a
total indifference, as you shewed at
Windsor, whichever you like best: the

barge is ready, and out you all set, full of
the highest joy and good-humour: you
have a fine day before you; it is agreed,
that you are to dine at Richmond, and to
walk in the gardens there: then the closing
your expedition with Ranelagh and Vauxhall in the evening, gives, in imagination,
the highest delight to the younger part
of your company; but, in imagination
alone, shall they enjoy either that, or
Richmond gardens, if you manage right.
Before you reach Kingston, you may be
suddenly taken with such a panic upon
the water, that, you may say, you never
felt before; you may scream at every
stroke of the oar; and, in short, when
you come to Twickenham, beg and intreat
your husband to let you get out, and tra-
vel home by land; for such an unaccountable terror of the water had seized
you, that you could not go any farther for
the world. Appear so very ill with the
fright, that it is proper, at least, for one

of your sisters to go ashore with you. But
here the fear is, that the rest of the company, being four of them, may pursue
their design, and leave you, your husband,
and sister, to get home as you can. Give
a hint, therefore, to your husband, that,
in about an hour, perhaps, when you have
drank a dish of tea with some drops, you
may possibly recover yourself enough to
pursue your first design; and, by this
means, you may get them all ashore.
Now never leave, till you have set on foot
some wrangling dispute or other, that
shall sour the whole company, and put
them off from every thought of pleasure.
It is most likely, that, on this, the young
lady whom you the first day turned out
of the chaise from her lover, having felt
from your wayward humours so many
disappointments, and not having the same
restraint as your husband's sisters, will
make a sort of mutiny, and will rebel
against your power: if so, you must exert

so much spleen and ill-nature towards her,
that the young gentleman will not forbear
taking her part. Now the sport begins!
for she, encouraged by having a knight
errant to defend her cause, will grow
pretty saucy; and you, knowing your fond
husband will support you in it, may increase in your insolence towards her. If
you and the young lady are both women
of spirit, and the young fellow and your
husband are both men of honour, an appointment is made behind Montagu-
house, and your party of pleasure ends in
a party of tilting; and, like Chevy-chase,
" the child may rue, that is unborn, the
" PLEASURE of that day."

THERE yet remain various connections,
that give fair opportunities for the exercise of our art; but it is presumed and
hoped, that there may be general instructions enough collected from my foregoing principal heads, to make a minute

enumeration of every such connection unnecessary. But——

Let all men in power be insolent to their dependents.

Let gaol-keepers be cruel to their prisoners.

Let the frequency of corporal punishments, and the unfrequency of rewarding men for long and faithful services, shew, that our science flourishes in military management.

Let the schoolmaster (since nothing lies open to him but the rod) spare not the birch, while custom indulges him in such a smart exercise of his authority.

In all other stations, a sharp and acute wit may, I doubt not, hit on some effectual method for making somebody or other miserable.

Or, should you be so unfortunate, as to have no human creature any way your dependent, you have, at least, the whole race of the domestic brute creation, on whom to wreak your malice.

One subject of your power, indeed, yet remains; and such a one as it is not in the art of man to deprive you of—

I mean YOURSELF.—Nor can any rank or degree of men who are my followers, supply my train with a larger company, than the race of SELF-TORMENTORS. In this class may be ranked the generality of old bachelors, and old maids; for this very good reason, that they can seldom find any creature who has regard enough for them to be hurt by their ill-humour, but THEMSELVES.

CONCLUSION OF THE ESSAY.

THAT great emperor Marcus Antoninus, in those excellent reflections which he has left to the world, declares, that he learnt such a precept from one person, and such a precept from another: Give me leave so far to follow his example, as modestly to disclaim the honour of invention in most of the foregoing rules, especially in those which appear the most exquisite and refined; for nothing but experience and observation could have convinced me, that the practice of some of them was possible.

So very delicate is this ingenious art of tormenting, that it is not obvious to vulgar eyes, in what manner it is most feelingly inflicted. For this reason it is, that rustic Jobson, when his wife offends him, takes the strap; and where the strength of arm is with the wife, she generally uses it in a manner to excite her neighbours to lampoon her by a Skimmington. But I have done my endeavour to set this matter in a clear light, throughout every chapter of my second division.

I once heard a lady declare, that she carefully concealed from her *friends* every thing she disliked, as she knew that to be the only chance she had for not being teazed and plagued with every little thing that was disagreeable to her. And can any one, from experience, contradict her prudence, founded, no doubt, on just observation? How have I seen a whole company made uneasy, from the screeching of a cork between some persons fingers! the constant drumming upon the table, or shaking of the knee, of another! the hawking and spawlting of a third! with various inventions of disagreeableness for offending some or all of the senses!

To rise a little higher—It is not your violent quarrels, or downright brutal sayings,
which sometimes pass in company, that
you have reason to fear; it is your sly,
malicious reflections, and invidious turns,
that may be given to well-meant words,
that makes company frequently very disagreeable. The lion and the tiger come
not often in our way; or if they did, we
should be aware of their teeth and claws;
but it is your gnats, your wasps, and, in
some countries, your musketo-flies, that
are your constant and true tormentors.

I know that many learned and good
men have taken great pains to undermine
this our noble art, by laying down rules,
and giving exemplars, in order to teach
mankind to give no offence to any one,
and, instead of being a torment, to be as
great a help and comfort to their friends,
as it is in their power to be. But with
infinite pleasure do I perceive, either that
they are not much read, or, at least, that

they have not the power of rooting from
the human breast that growing sprig, of
mischief there implanted with our birth;
and generally, as we come to years of dis-
cretion, flourishing like a green palm-tree:
yet, to shew my great candour and generosity to these my mortal (or rather moral)
foes, I will endeavour, as far as my poor
recommendation will go, to forward the
sale of their books, even among my own
pupils. For if, my good scholars, you will
guard your minds against the doctrines
they intend to teach; if you will consider
them as mere amusements; you have my
leave to peruse them. Or rather, if you
will only remember to observe my orders,
in acting in direct opposition to all that a
Swift, an Addison, a Richardson, a Fielding, or any other good ethical writer intended to teach, you may (by referring
sometimes to these my rules, as helps to
your memory) become as profound adepts
in this art, as any of the readers of Mr.
Hoyle are in the science of whist.

Great are the disputes amongst the learned, whether man, as an animal, be a savage and ferocious, or a gentle and social beast. Swift's picture, in his Yahoes, gives us not a very favourable view of the natural disposition of the animal man; yet I remember not, that he supposes him naturally to delight in tormenting; or does he make him guilty of any vices, but following his brutish appetites. Must not this love of tormenting, therefore, be cultivated and cherished? There are many tastes, as that of the olive, the oyster, with several high sauces, cooked up with assafœtida and the like, which at first are disgustful to the palate, but when once a man has so far depraved his natural taste, as to get a relish for those dainties, there is nothing he is half so fond of.

I can recollect but one kind of brute, that seems to have any notion of this pleasant practice of tormenting; and that is the cat, when she has got a mouse— She delays the gratification of her hunger, which prompted her to seek for food, and triumphs in her power over her wretched captive—She not only sticks her claws into it, making it feel the sharpness of her teeth (without touching the vitals enough to render it insensible to her tricks), but she tosses it over her head in sport, seems in the highest joy imaginable, and is also, to all appearance, at that very time, the sweetest best-humoured animal in the world. Yet should any thing approach her, that she fears will rob her of her play-thing (holding her prey fast in her teeth), she swears, she growls, and shews all the savage motions of her heart. As soon as her fears are over, she again resumes her sport; and is, in this one instance only, kinder to her victim, than her imitators man, that by death she at last puts a final end to the poor wretch's torments.

Was I to rack my invention and memory for ever, I could not find a more adequate picture of the true lovers of tormenting than this sportive cat: nor will I tire my reader's patience longer, than to add this one farther precept:

REMEMBER ALWAYS TO DO UNTO EVERY ONE, WHAT YOU WOULD LEAST WISH TO HAVE DONE UNTO YOURSELF; for in this is contained the whole of our excellent SCIENCE.

A FABLE.

In the time when beasts could speak, and write, and read the English language, and were moved with the same passions as men; there was found an old poem, in which was strongly described the misery that is endured, from the entrance of teeth and claws into living flesh. In the strongest colours was painted the pain which the poor sufferer sustains, his agonizing faintness from loss of blood, with the exquisite torment he undergoes, until his heart-felt anguish is relieved by death.

The name of the author was not prefixed to this poem; but on the title-page, at the bottom, was inscribed the letter L.

Its real author not being known, a claim (in the name of their ancestors) was laid to it by all the savage race. The critics take the matter in hand, and endless would have been the debate, had not the letter L, on the title-page, confined the competitors to the lion, the leopard, the lynx, and the lamb.

The lamb, by almost general consent, was instantly thrown out, as knowing nothing of the subjects treated of in the poem. Long were the pleadings of the lion, the leopard, and the lynx, to prove, from the strength of the one, the activity of the other, and the fierceness of the third, that each was best qualified for writing a pathetic description: till at last the generous horse begged leave to observe—That the poem now contended for, could not be the work of any one of the above claimants, who had roared so loud to prove their title: " For it is im-
" possible (says he), that any beast, that
" has the feeling which our author shews
" for the tortured wretches, who are torn
" by savage teeth and claws, should ever

" make the ravages, which, it is notorious,
" are daily made by the three fierce com-
" petitors before us. The writer of this
" poem, therefore, (continued he), must
" be no other than the lamb. As it is
" from suffering, and not from inflicting
" torments, that the true idea of them is
" gained."

Printed by W. Bulmer and Co,
Cleveland-row, St. James's.

Lightning Source UK Ltd.
Milton Keynes UK
UKOW05f2146061015

259947UK00008B/150/P